Aeschylus: Eumenides

D1523599

KU-483-704

DUCKWORTH COMPANIONS
TO GREEK AND ROMAN TRAGEDY

Series editor: Thomas Harrison

DUCKWORTH COMPANIONS
TO GREEK AND ROMAN TRAGEDY

Aeschylus: Eumenides

Robin Mitchell-Boyask

Duckworth

First published in 2009 by
Gerald Duckworth & Co. Ltd.
90-93 Cowcross Street, London EC1M 6BF
Tel: 020 7100 7300
Fax: 020 7490 0080
info@duckworth-publishers.co.uk
www.ducknet.co.uk

A catalogue record for this book is available
from the British Library

ISBN 978 0 7156 3642 8

Typeset by Ray Davies
Printed and bound in Great Britain by
CPI Antony Rowe, Chippenham and Eastbourne

Contents

Acknowledgements

I first read the *Oresteia* as an undergraduate at the University of Chicago. I did not like it. Only late in my graduate course work with the late Charles Segal at Brown did I start to appreciate the genius of Aeschylus, but my true scholarly passions continued to lie elsewhere. It was only when I had taught the *Oresteia* several times and started to devote more energy to Page's OCT that I realized that Aeschylus was indeed right: we learn by suffering! This book is a peace offering to the now lost tomb of Aeschylus in Sicily. I must first thank Aeschylus for composing a trilogy so magnificent it took three Duckworth Companions to do it justice.

Aside from Segal, I have been fortunate to have the opportunity to discuss *Eumenides* with two other great scholars, Pat Easterling and Richard Seaford. With the latter I enjoyed a most spirited debate on the trial scene at the 2007 annual meeting of the Classical Association of the United Kingdom in Birmingham. Earlier conversations with Peter Meineck about the Aeschylean stagecraft changed the way I think about Greek drama. My work on this book has come during a most productive period that has been enriched, if not enabled, by the friendship of Douglas Cairns, Andromache Karanika, Sheila B. Murnaghan, and Robin Osborne.

I laid the groundwork for this study in 2005 during a very happy term as a Visiting Fellow at Wolfson College, Cambridge University, where I had the good fortune to spend many hours in the library of the Classics Faculty. Thanks again to Pat Easterling and Robin Osborne for making that experience possible. I am further grateful for a release from teaching duties during the winter of 2008 from Temple University's College of Liberal Arts that allowed me the kind of sustained focus required to finish a book.

Tom Harrison's confidence in me was, and continues to be, a source of strength. I hope I have rewarded his trust. Thanks also to Deborah Blake at Duckworth for her help and for her patience.

Preface

Eumenides tells the story of Orestes' salvation from punishment by the Furies for murdering his mother, Clytemnestra, through the institution of trial by jury in Athens. The third and concluding drama in Aeschylus' sole surviving trilogy, the *Oresteia*, it continues to be not just one of the most admired Greek tragedies, but also one of the most controversial and contested, both to specialist scholars and public intellectuals. My own conclusion about *Eumenides* after completing this book is that it just might be the most contested of all Greek tragedies. Scholars argue about what and who is in the acting area (and when and how), about how many people are in the jury, what their vote is, what Athena actually does, and what the acquiescence of the Furies means. As should become apparent in my detailed discussion of the play, one source of these controversies is the sheer level of innovation and experimentation that Aeschylus attempts in *Eumenides*. Aeschylus deploys new dramatic and theatrical tools and techniques, and he works hard to keep his audience off its guard.

In this volume I shall examine in detail the political, social and dramatic contexts of *Eumenides* and important issues that the drama addresses, such as justice and gender conflict. My goal is to synthesize much of the important scholarship on *Eumenides* from the past three decades that have seen so much progress in our understanding of Aeschylus, while also imparting my own readings of some of the most contested aspects of the *Oresteia*'s third part. I shall try to make *Eumenides* feel like a piece of living theatre by paying attention to performance

9

issues, but in a way that keeps its political and social aspects vibrantly relevant.

All translations of Aeschylus are my own, unless otherwise specified. I discuss the relative merits of the available translations in the Suggestions for Further Reading. In this study I have made use of, and thus cite, Sommerstein's outstanding Greek text and commentary. Anyone writing on *Eumenides* now owes an enormous debt to the commentaries of Sommerstein and Podlecki.

1

Aeschylus the Athenian

This chapter presents an overview of the career of Aeschylus, set against the birth of Athenian democracy during his teens and the two wars against Persia in which Aeschylus fought. I shall here discuss Aeschylus' contributions to the development of tragic drama in Athens and how his dramas, especially the *Oresteia*, are understood as participating in the development of Athenian democracy and its institutions.

The facts of the lives of the ancient Greek poets must always be considered with great caution, for they frequently derive from anecdotes from late antiquity that are an unreliable (though often amusing) mixture of speculation, gossip, folk tale and motifs derived from the poems themselves.[1] One such story from the ancient *Life* involves the first performance of *Eumenides* itself: so terrifying were the Furies' costumes that the pregnant women in the audience miscarried when they first caught sight of them. Now, all of the characters in Aeschylus' *Eumenides* comment on the Furies' loathsome appearance, so a particularly violent reaction from its first audience seems quite probable, but not this particular reaction: women were either not present in the theatre at all, or, if they did attend, they probably sat at the back where the sheer size of the Theatre of Dionysus would probably have made the details of the chorus' costumes less compelling.[2] The death of Aeschylus also receives an amusing treatment in the biographical legends: Aeschylus, during his final trip to Sicily, met his end when an eagle, which was carrying a turtle and seeking a rock on which to smash its shell, mistakenly hurled it down at Aeschylus' bald head and struck him dead. Turtles are popular figures in Greek folk tales and eagles figure prominently in Aeschylus' *Agamemnon*, so this story, while certainly possible, sounds more suspicious than others. Nonetheless, the death of Aeschylus in Gela, Sicily does seem a reliable item.

Aeschylus and the birth of democracy in Athens

Aside from the manner of his death, other details of Aeschylus' life are fairly trustworthy, and the story of his life is very much the story of Athens' rise. His late adolescence and adult prime saw the two seminal events in the ascent of Athens: the beginning of democracy and the wars against Persia. He was born, son of Euphorion, probably in 525/24 BC to an aristocratic family at Eleusis, a town roughly fourteen miles northwest of Athens. The celebrations of the Eleusinian Mysteries, the great religious festival in honour of the goddess Demeter and her daughter Persephone, filled Aeschylus' childhood with the rituals and myths of the great goddesses of fertility, death and renewal. At the time of his birth, dramas were still being performed in the Athenian Agora. The dramas themselves consisted of choral songs about a hero or god and a single, masked actor who stepped forward to represent the main character. This was the institution of the semi-legendary first dramatist, Thespis, in the decade before Aeschylus' birth. During the time of Thespis' activities, the Athenian tyrant Peisistratus transformed an older festival in honour of the god Dionysus into the City Dionysia. Peisistratus also reorganized the Panathenaia, a quadrennial Athenian festival, into a Pan-Hellenic event, with processions, athletic competitions, and, most importantly for the young Aeschylus, recitations of Homeric epic and performances of choral poetry by poets such as Simonides and solo lyric performances by the likes of Anacreon. Athens was well on its way to being a hotbed of poetic performance and innovation.

The pace of change in Athens accelerated towards the end of the sixth century. In 508 Cleisthenes, riding a wave of popular support, routed the governing aristocrats, and instituted the democracy that characterized Athens for the next century.[3] Thus, when Aeschylus was seventeen, *dêmokratia*, the rule of the people, was born, but its full gestation would take the rest of his life and become one of the underlying concerns of his *Eumenides*. Roughly ten years after democratic rule began in Athens, the dramatic performances of the City Dionysia, in which Aeschylus was already competing, moved from the Agora to the south slope of the Acropolis. The city of Athens and its theatre thus, early in the adulthood of Aeschylus, took the forms he would inhabit, save for his trips to Sicily, for the rest of his life.[4] His plays, which would fundamentally transform the theatre, are also important documents for understanding the development of Athens in the first half of the fifth century BC. Indeed, it is in one of Aeschylus' tragedies, *Suppliants*, that one finds the first surviving cluster of words that forms our word democracy: *dêmou kratousa cheir* (604, 'the ruling hand of the people').

If the decisive moment in Athenian internal affairs was the Cleisthenic revolution of 508 BC, the international watershed for Athens came when the Persians invaded Greece, eventually occupying Athens itself. In 499, around the time Athenian dramatic performances moved to the south slope of the Acropolis and Aeschylus began his career, along Asia Minor's west coast a number of Greek cities that had been incorporated forcibly into the Persian Empire revolted against their master. It took the Persians five years to crush this rebellion, which was eventually supported by Athens. In 490 BC the Persian King Darius used this Athenian assistance as an excuse to assault the heart of Greece itself. Against their second incursion, at Marathon, Aeschylus fought, and the often unreliable *Life* (10) records that he arranged for the following epitaph for his tomb in Sicily:

This monument in wheat-growing Gela conceals an Athenian dead man: Aeschylus, son of Euphorion. Of his noble courage the sacred field of Marathon can tell, and the longhaired Mede, who had good cause to know.

It may well be surprising to a modern reader that Aeschylus did not want to be remembered first and foremost as the greatest tragic poet of his day, but rather as a simple, brave Athenian soldier. The pivotal battle at Salamis, at which Aeschylus also most probably fought, ended Persian hopes for the conquest of Greece. In full view of Darius' successor Xerxes, the Athenian fleet destroyed the Persians, thus essentially ending the Persian threat. In 472 BC Aeschylus would mount his historical drama about the battle of Salamis and its aftermath, *Persians*.[5]

War's presence in the surviving works of Aeschylus reflects the realities of his age and his personal experience. Aeschylus was well aware of the more mundane, even seedier, aspects of conflict, as shown in the Herald's reports in *Agamemnon* (551-82) of the Greek army's decade of suffering. He was also aware, again as is shown throughout *Agamemnon*, of the terrible price paid by individuals for interstate conflict, and of the fact that motives for war are often questionable. Yet he had also seen his city win great battles repeatedly and experienced their glory and the spoils of victory; hence, at the close of *Eumenides*, the goddess Athena, in words that often startle and annoy modern readers, seems to be a great cheerleader for the future wars that Athens will wage (864-65, 913-15).

Domestic tyranny came to an end in 508 and Persian invasion was over by 479 BC, but they never lost their grip on the Athenian, and Aeschylean, imagination during the succeeding decades. In the Athenian theatre Persians become 'the barbarian', the repository of all that is feared and uncivilized.[6] As late as 422 BC, Aristophanes' comic masterpiece *Wasps* portrayed a risible degree of paranoia about tyranny, showing how deeply fearful popular consciousness remained of its return.[7] The twin fears of Persia and tyranny actively shaped Aeschylus' *Oresteia* in 458 BC. Troy, located on the northwest coast of Asia Minor, falls as the trilogy opens, and seems assimilated to Persia, especially in the portrait of Agamemnon who, on his return, acts like a debauched autocratic ruler who has gone native during his decade in Troy/Persia. Following his death, *Libation Bearers* represents the rule of Clytemnestra and Aegisthus in

14

Argos as a tyranny that Orestes overthrows. *Eumenides* then glances at recent Athenian battles near Troy (397-402) and engagements with Persian forces in Libya (289-96), and its core, the trial of Orestes, seems to have something to do with current concerns about further protecting Athenian democracy. The location of Orestes' trial, the Areopagus ('the hill of Ares') becomes (685-90) the camp from which the tribe of warrior women, the Amazons, launched their attack on Theseus and Athens; this allusion would doubtless have been designed to trigger Athenian memory that the Persians also used the Areopagus as a base to attack the Acropolis, especially since Amazons were conceptually linked with Persians in Athenian thought.[8] Some time in the decade after the *Oresteia*'s production and the death of Aeschylus, during the absolute height of Athenian imperial power, Pericles, the great Athenian politician and general, would build adjacent to the Theatre of Dionysus an enclosed music hall, his Odeion, whose pyramidal roof imitated that of a Persian tent. The environs of the Theatre of Dionysus, the artistic home of Aeschylus, thus became part of the commemoration of the Athenian defeat of Xerxes.[9] As Aristophanes' *Frogs* shows, Aeschylean tragedy itself will, at the end of the fifth century, late in the Peloponnesian War, come to signify the Athens that was able to bring down the greatest power the world had known.

The career of Aeschylus

Aeschylus, like his successors Sophocles and Euripides, was a prolific dramatist, composing between 82 and 90 individual plays. A catalogue transmitted by several medieval manuscripts of the seven surviving plays list 73 titles, but at least nine more were known to ancient scholars. The *Suda*, an encyclopaedia of antiquity from the Byzantine era, credits him with 90. Since Athenian playwrights did not produce their dramas individually, but in groups of four at the City Dionysia, Aeschylus must have competed there roughly 22 times. He probably made his debut in 499/98 (or 496) and won his first victory in

484, but his earliest surviving tragedy, *Persians*, dates from 472, when he was a mature artist in his early 50s. Of his 82 or 90 plays, only seven survive (or six, if, as most now believe, *Prometheus Bound* was either only in part by Aeschylus or wholly by another, now anonymous poet); aside from *Prometheus Bound*, we have the three dramas of the *Oresteia*, *Persians*, *Suppliants*, and *Seven against Thebes*.[10]

Save for *Persians*, all of the surviving works attributed to Aeschylus are believed to have been parts of tetralogies, four plays performed in sequence on the same programme and related in plot.[11] Each poet who competed in the City Dionysia presented not just three tragedies, but also a satyr play, a comic burlesque that is generally believed to have lampooned the preceding more serious trio. Aeschylus was renowned for his satyr plays. The *Oresteia* is commonly known as a trilogy because its satyr play, *Proteus*, has been lost. *Proteus* depicted the efforts of Agamemnon's brother Menelaus in Egypt to secure information from the shape-shifting sea god Proteus, an episode found in Homer's *Odyssey* (4.351-75).[12] Aeschylus, who may have invented the tetralogic form, composed tetralogies at least ten of the 22 times he competed. This seems to have been his preferred mode of composition, since it afforded him the large canvas on which he could depict his great themes of justice, societal change and the evolution of the *kosmos*.[13] The loss of the plays that accompanied *Suppliants*, *Seven against Thebes* and *Prometheus Bound* certainly cripples our ability to understand their survivors.

The success of Aeschylus both at home and abroad was considerable. Ancient testimonials report that he had either 13 or 28 victories; the latter total must include posthumous victories, but the run of 13 victories in 22 tries is a remarkable achievement in itself. His fame and curiosity about the world brought him at least twice to Sicily, the western edge of the Greek world, which, while it lacked the political ferment of Athenian democracy, was still a worthy cultural rival to Aeschylus' home.

Some time between 472 and 468 Aeschylus was invited to the

court of Hieron I at Syracuse to revive his prize-winning *Persae*, and, in honour of the new city of Aetna, which Hieron had built at the volcano's foot, Aeschylus produced his *Aetnaetae* or *The Women of Aetna* (now lost). Sicily and Hieron's court were during this decade a centre of learning and literature, frequented by leading philosophers (Xenophanes and Empedocles), and poets (Aeschylus' colleague the early dramatist Phrynicus, Simonides and perhaps Pindar). After this invigorating experience Aeschylus returned to Athens, and found himself in 468 defeated by Sophocles, then only 28 years old and making his debut. Plutarch's *Life of Cimon* (8) tells a story (which, again, may or may not be true) that the audience argued so bitterly about this competition that Cimon and several other generals were called upon to adjudicate, replacing the chosen judges. Cimon, we shall see, figures in the political background of Aeschylus' *Eumenides*. Plutarch goes on to say that an annoyed Aeschylus then left Athens for Sicily forever, which, of course, would have made the *Oresteia*'s production ten years later somewhat difficult. Sometime after his victory with the *Oresteia* and the fall of the Sicilian tyrants, Aeschylus returned to Sicily and died at Gela in 456.

The evidence suggests not an angry aging artist, but an Aeschylus reinvigorated by his Sicilian experience and the challenge from the younger Sophocles. From the decade following his defeat by Sophocles, we retain five of his plays, all of them victorious. From the years between the production of *Persians* in 472 and his death in 456, we know of 24 plays composed by Aeschylus, who was also quick to adapt innovations by Sophocles and others. Aristotle tells us that Sophocles introduced the third actor and scenery (*Poetics* 1449a19). It is not clear from Aristotle's skeletal comments whether 'scenery' means the use of the small building at the back of the acting area (*skênê*) or simply the painting of it. As we shall see in the next chapter, Aeschylus either instituted the *skênê* for the *Oresteia*, or took it over from a contemporary and quickly made it his own from the *Oresteia*'s opening lines. It is generally believed that Sophocles began to use a third actor only shortly

17

before the *Oresteia*'s production, since Aeschylus deploys him so sparingly in its first two plays, though to great effect.[14] In *Eumenides*, Aeschylus clearly commands the use of three speaking actors, although during the trial Apollo, Orestes and Athena tend each to address mainly the chorus and jury and not the other two actors.

Aeschylus thus intensifies his work late in life, in the context of intellectual and cultural ferment. His decision to return to Sicily shows a man eager for new experiences and knowledge, working at the peak of his powers until the unexpected end, whether it came as a result of an eagle and a turtle, or something more dignified.

Aeschylus' successful career even extended beyond his natural life. So great was his reputation that his works received the unique privilege of new productions in dramatic competitions after his death. His two sons, Euphorion and Euaeon, became poets in their own right after their father's death, and the former is said to have won four victories with his father's work. His nephew Philocles beat the Sophoclean programme that included *Oedipus Tyrannus* and founded a theatrical dynasty that endured for a century. Aristophanes' comedy, *Frogs*, which dates from the end of the fifth century, ended with the god Dionysus returning Aeschylus from the Underworld to Athens to save the city through his art. Aristophanes aside, the theatrical activities of his family members and new performances of his works provided Aeschylus with some form of life after death.

The *Eumenides* and Greek Myth and Religion

This chapter looks at the mythic and religious materials available to Aeschylus in composing *Oresteia*'s ultimate tragic part. It is important to remember that, while Greek tragic playwrights almost invariably mined heroic myth for their plots, they enjoyed a fair amount of freedom in shaping these myths to their needs, and the audience did not necessarily know what would happen. Surprise, I shall show later, played a key role in Aeschylus' art. In this chapter I examine first the myths of the Furies' pursuit of Orestes and his trial before Aeschylus, then the nature of the Furies, and finally the conflict between the gods in *Eumenides*.[1]

The myths at the heart of Aeschylus' drama fall into groups: (1) what happens to Orestes after the matricide, and (2) the foundation myth for the Areopagus council in Athens. The Furies join these two areas together. A new reader (or, if lucky, spectator) of *Eumenides* would imagine that the Furies' pursuit and the Athenian trial must be unalterable aspects of the legend of Orestes, and, while even a casual reading of Homeric epic shows important references to Orestes and to the Furies, yet nowhere does Homer mention Furies and Orestes together. I discuss the Homeric Furies in the next section of this chapter, but first I turn to Orestes in Homer and Homer's successors.

Orestes

Homer handles Orestes with great care. The story of Orestes avenging his father by killing his mother's lover Aegisthus forms the mythological paradigm for Odysseus' son Telemachus in the *Odyssey's* first four books. Homer tells this tale four times through four different narrators (1.40-1, 1.298-300, 3.193-8, 4.512-40), and its basic shape remains the same each time: Orestes kills his father's murderer, and there is almost no mention of Clytemnestra. Homer suppresses matricide when he is most concerned with establishing the justice of killing Penelope's suitors and with Telemachus' maturation.[2] But once Odysseus becomes the narrative's main character in Book 5, Clytemnestra begins to peek in around the edges. The ghost of Agamemnon himself, aware of his own murder but not of his son's vengeance, tells Odysseus in the Underworld about his death, but the focus then suddenly shifts to Clytemnestra (11.405-34). The epithet that had characterized Aegisthus earlier, 'deceptively clever' (1.300, and again at 3.308), now applies to Clytemnestra. Aegisthus remains Agamemnon's murderer, but Clytemnestra kills Cassandra, as she does in Aeschylus. When the souls of Penelope's suitors descend to Hades, the shift to Clytemnestra accelerates. Agamemnon hears of the deeds of Penelope and Odysseus and, after praising the former, again denounces Clytemnestra, but with even greater vehemence, who 'contrived evil deeds, / and killed her husband' (24.199-200). Aegisthus has disappeared and Clytemnestra now seems the mastermind. This approaches Aeschylean territory, but, if Clytemnestra has turned out to be at least as blameworthy as Aegisthus, one would expect some account of the consequences of her treachery. Nestor does refer to a funeral feast for Aegisthus and Clytemnestra after reporting that Orestes killed the former – but not the latter (3.310)! Unless Clytemnestra simply dropped dead in shock at Aegisthus' demise, Orestes must have killed her. The one Homeric hint of Orestes' experiences *after* his vengeance comes when Nestor relates 'godlike Orestes came from Athens and killed his father's murderer, / deceptively clever Aegisthus' (3.306-8). The combination of this reference to a visit to Athens, out of sequence from other versions, in the same passage as the only Homeric allusion to matricide, suggests the possibility that Homer knew a myth in which Orestes fled to Athens after killing his mother.

2. The Eumenides and Greek Myth and Religion

For other anticipations of Aeschylus' Oresteian myth we must look elsewhere. The Hesiodic *Catalogue of Women* (fragment 23) portrays an Orestes 'who grew to manhood and paid back his father's slayer and slew his over-bearing mother with pitiless bronze'. In the century before Aeschylus, Stesichorus composed an Oresteian poem that probably had Apollo command the matricide. Simonides (around 500 BC) followed Stesichorus in involving Apollo. Closer to the production of Aeschylus' *Oresteia*, Pindar's *Pythian* 11 (474 BC) contains hints of Apollo's role, as he mentions Orestes' exile in the house of Pylades at the foot of Parnassus, which is located near Delphi (36), thus giving an Apollonian frame to the story. Pindar, however, as he reaches the matricide, claims Ares helped Orestes (36-7) and then suddenly changes subject and avoids discussion of matricide. Thus, as one approaches Aeschylus, the matricide and Apollo's role in it both loom larger. Some time around the composition of the *Oresteia*, Herodotus writes in his *History* (1.67) the story of the Spartan recovery of Orestes' bones on the instructions of the Pythia, who insists that the Spartans can never defeat the Tegeans without the help of these bones; this story, which Aeschylus might have known in some form, clearly refers to the hero cult (albeit in Argos, not Sparta) that Orestes announces will help the Athenians (*Eumenides* 767-74) in their future wars.[3] There is thus a link with Delphi and Apollo, but no mention of Orestes' career.

Myth and the Areopagus

The very name Areopagus, 'the rock of Ares', suggests some kind of foundation myth. But if we take into account not just the physical rock but also the human institution named after it, there are in fact two separate foundation myths, both involving a murder trial, only one of which features Orestes. Moreover, the Areopagus' role in the defence of Athens by the mythical hero Theseus against the invading Amazons and, in history, against the Persian forces, combined with its location as the trial of Orestes, make it key element in Athenian self-definition.

21

The mound was named after Ares when the war god killed Halirrothius, Poseidon's son, who had raped Ares' daughter. A divine jury tried Ares there, as attested by sources later than Aeschylus (e.g. Euripides, *Electra* 1258-62; *Iphigenia at Tauris* 945-6; Apollodorus 3.14.2). In *Eumenides*, Athena does not mention her half-brother's trial, but the rock's name itself may well have sufficed to recall the earlier myth. Other mythical trials quickly became attached to the Areopagus, such as Cephalus' for killing his wife Procris and Daedalus' for murdering his nephew Talos, but it is uncertain when these stories arose relative to Aeschylus' *Eumenides*.

Thus the trial of Orestes at Athens and on the Areopagus is just one of several murder trials to have taken place there, albeit the most famous one. As we saw earlier, Orestes was already associated with Athens in some vague way as early as Homer's *Odyssey* (3.306-10), and this association becomes stronger in the light of ritual practices on Choes, the second day of the Athenian Dionysian festival of Anthesteria. On Choes, Athenians believed, the souls of the dead would ascend from Hades. Athenians would then sit silently and drink wine from individual cups, in contrast to the convivial shared drinking of the symposium. The aetiological myth for this event was Orestes' visit to Athens in order to receive purification. But his pollution prevented him from communing with other men in hospitality rituals. To avoid embarrassment and the violation of the codes of *xenia* (ritualized guest-friendship), either the Athenian king or her people declared that everyone celebrating this festival should be silent and not share cups. In *Eumenides* (448) Orestes might allude to Choes as he refers to laws that forbid speech by a murderer who has not been cleansed ritually. In a drama that is key to the *Oresteia*'s reception, *Iphigenia at Tauris*, Orestes explains his Athenian welcome (947-60). The Choes ritual would thus seem to depend on an ancient myth of Orestes' trial in Athens at the Areopagus which Aeschylus then chooses as the basis for resolving the tribulations of the House of Atreus in his *Oresteia*.

There seems to have been three forms of the myth of Orestes' trial on which Aeschylus drew selectively and then transformed. One can divide the three streams according to differences among prosecutors, judges and results.[4] Orestes' prosecutors were the Furies or their cousins, the Semnai Theai ('the August Goddesses'), or the relatives of Clytemnestra and Aegisthus. The judges were a human panel or a jury of gods.[5] All sources have Orestes acquitted, but differ on the manner of it. Only half indicate the equal vote (e.g. Euripides, *Electra* 1265-6; *Iphigenia at Tauris* 965-6, 1470-2), and only *Iphigenia at Tauris* 965-6 and Aristides (*Orations* 37.17) mention the role of Athena. Moreover, only Euripides' *Electra* (1266-7) and *Iphigenia at Tauris* (965) include Apollo's testimony as a factor.

Thus, Aeschylus changes the prosecutor from human to divine and, in the other direction, the jury from divine to human. It is credible that there were pre-Aeschylean versions of the myth in which the prosecutor's identity varied, but Aeschylus seems so concerned to dramatize the establishment of the Areopagus tribunal that one is led to conclude that the human jury was probably his innovation. Moreover, as we shall see shortly, his conception of the Furies seems so original that it is more likely that he also invented their identity as the prosecutors. Since Apollo could not be both a witness to the court and a part of the jury, the former must also be Aeschylus' idea, as was Athena's ordination of the acquittal by equal votes.

The Furies

Erinyes, Furies, Eumenides, Semnai Theai. The dark goddesses who pursue Orestes in Aeschylus either receive these names or are closely linked to them. What to call these figures must be considered before discussing what, exactly, they are, for their name is strangely problematic. As I shall show later, the name 'Furies' becomes significant in the *Oresteia*'s course by its gradual withdrawal. Our word 'Furies' derives from a Latin verb of anger, and, while it appropriately designates the nature and activities of the punishers of matricide, one must be aware that the Greeks had another word for them: Erinyes.

23

'Erinyes' has never had much currency in translations of Greek literature, since 'Furies' communicates instantly, and 'Erinyes' seems almost unpronounceable (Er-in-ooh-ehs), if not meaningless. The name, however, is considerably ancient and appears in a Linear B tablet from Knossos; it thus goes back at least as far as the Mycenaean civilization. Moreover, the verb *erinuein* in Arcadian means to be angry (Pausanias 8.25.6), though it could be based on the name Erinyes.[6] I, like most commentators on *Eumenides*, will continue to use their more common English name.

'Eumenides' presents its own problems. One would think that name given in the play's title would be relatively straightforward, but it certainly is not. 'Eumenides' means something like 'the fair-minded (or 'kindly') ones', and suggests their transformation from the angry goddesses of the vendetta to the enforcers of true justice in Athens. But the word itself never appears in the surviving text of Aeschylus' play. The relevant lines possibly dropped out during transmission, but scholarly consensus has moved away from this solution.[7] Indeed, the word 'Eumenides' appears only in ancillary materials in the manuscripts, and there is no evidence that the play was known by this title in the fifth century. The name 'Eumenides' seems to have begun to be used only in the late fifth century, and it is not unknown for translators to call the trilogy's final part *The Furies* (so Meineck's translation).[8] Since in Euripides' *Orestes*, set before his trial, Orestes' pursuers are called Eumenides four times (38, 321, 836, 1650) and Erinyes four times (238, 264, 582, 1389), the two names seem to have become interchangeable by that play's production in 408 BC, 50 years after the *Oresteia*. But in *Iphigenia at Tauris*, produced only six years earlier in 414, they are named only as Erinyes, nine times (79, 294, 299, 931, 963, 970, 1439, 1456). If the texts of Greek tragedy indicate social reality in some meaningful way, then the two Euripidean dramas signal some kind of shift in Athenian religious terminology.

But Aeschylus might intend the Furies to be transformed not into the Eumenides, but into their cousins, the Semnai Theai,

2. The Eumenides *and Greek Myth and Religion*

the August Goddesses. At the end of *Eumenides*, Athena even explicitly calls her new allies 'Semnai' (1041). The cult described by Athena in the *Oresteia*'s final moments bears a strong resemblance to the cult of the Semnai Theai, who were worshipped in a cave close to the Areopagus, on the side nearer to the Acropolis. Their cult, unlike that of the Aeschylean Furies, was particularly known for providing sanctuary to suppliants.[9] Like the Furies at the end of the *Oresteia*, they were closely associated with the Areopagus Council and received sacrifices. Aeschylus was likely the first to identify the Semnai with the Erinyes, but not the first to associate the Semnai with the Areopagus, so Orestes' suppliancy in *Eumenides* would be discordant with identifying the two sets of goddesses. The power of Aeschylus' new synthesizing religious vision might even have spurred on or accelerated changes to Athenian cult, for, by the end of the fifth century, Furies, Eumenides and Semnai are indistinguishable from one another. But even during Aeschylus' own life these three groups were probably similar enough to allow for close association.[10]

Who, then, were these beings of Aeschylus' imagination and how did they relate to their earlier literary incarnations? It will become quickly clear that both the Furies' physical appearance and the restricting of their function to punishing the shedders of kindred blood were driven by Aeschylus' thematic and dramatic needs in *Eumenides*.[11] Let us start with a late source that mentions these problems in the context of the discrepancies between Aeschylus' vision of the Furies and those of his predecessors. While describing Athens, Pausanias (1.28.6) writes that near the place on the Areopagus where trials were held,

> there is a sanctuary of the goddesses whom the Athenians called Semnai, and whom Hesiod in the *Theogony* called Erinyes. Aeschylus was the first to represent them with snakes in their hair; but in their images, and in those of such other chthonic gods as are present, there is nothing terrible.

Vase paintings from the fifth and fourth centuries of Orestes' flight show female beings, with wings, sometimes gesturing angrily or chasing Orestes, but certainly nothing so terrible as to cause pregnant women to miscarry. The loathsome, dark, snake-covered, blood-dripping creatures are unique to Aeschylus' *Oresteia*.

Aeschylus' sources in Archaic poetry are not inconsistent with Aeschylus in their depiction of the Furies' functions; Aeschylus simply narrows them during their pursuit of Orestes and then broadens them again as the play winds down and the Furies are integrated into society. Murder, especially intra-familial murder, is the most fundamental disruption of structure and thus threatens chaos more than any other kind of action. In Homer and Hesiod the Furies seem most concerned with the preservation of order, whether that order is cosmic, societal, or familial. The messenger goddess Iris warns the potentially rebellious Poseidon about disobeying Zeus (*Iliad* 15.204): 'You know the Furies always follow the elder.' Their support for authority and age is consonant with a very frequent (and thus likely primary) association with the wronged parent's curse (*Iliad* 9.454, 9.571-2, 21.412; *Odyssey* 2.135, 11.280; Hesiod, *Theogony* 472). The Furies' enforcement of parental curse and their abode in darkness (*Iliad* 9.572) both recur in the Furies' first identification of themselves to Athena (*Eumenides* 416-17): 'we are named Curses in our homes beneath the earth'. Similarly, Pindar (*Olympian* 2.241) presents a Fury who sees Oedipus kill Laius and consequently makes Oedipus' sons destroy each other, the first representation of the Furies as visiting one generation's sins on the next. In Aeschylus' *Seven against Thebes* (572) the Furies continue to be identified with a parental curse, here Oedipus' on his sons. Hesiod's version of the Furies' birth from the rebellion of the son Kronos against his father Ouranos (*Theogony* 180-7) thus seems to establish permanently the prerogative of the Furies in enforcing the authority of the parent. While the Aeschylean Furies only designate their lineage as 'daughters of Night' (*Eumenides* 416), Aeschylus' larger concern with

Hesiod's cosmogonic myth likely keeps stories such as the castration of Ouranos in play.[12]

The Aeschylean Furies embody the civilizing force of the
protector of order, but they also could be identified, in their
violent threats to Orestes early in *Eumenides*, with the Keres,
bloodsucking, bestial death spirits (*Theogony* 213, 217, 220-2).
As Orestes' trial is about to begin, they sing about the urgency
of avoiding both anarchy and tyranny, and of keeping to the
mean (490-536). Their concern, continually, is with Justice
(511, 525, 539, 550, 554, 565), *dikê*, in its broadest sense, the
preservation of right and order. Their obsession with their role
in preserving order is completely consistent with Iris' warning
to Poseidon about the Furies' protection of the elder's rights. In
a drama possibly written by Aeschylus and certainly later than
the *Oresteia, Prometheus Bound*, the Titan Prometheus, as he
begins to hint of the potential fall of Zeus, responds to the
chorus' question, 'Who then is the helmsman of Necessity?',
with a further confirmation of the Furies' centrality: 'The tri-
form Fates (*Moirai*) and the remembering Furies' (515-16).

Furies and Olympians in Aeschylus'
Eumenides

In this section I sketch the development of the Oresteian Furies
from unseen angry spirits of vengeance in *Agamemnon* to the
visible agents of justice in Athens at the end of *Eumenides*. This
discussion will involve in its second half an examination of the
clash between Olympian and Chthonic deities in the trial of
Orestes.

First, I should say a few words about these categories of
Olympian and Chthonic.[13] *Chthonos* is the Greek word for
earth; so Chthonic deities are gods of the earth whose realms,
essentially, are death and fertility. It is a fairly simple move
then to incorporate related concepts such as punishment for
bloodshed and justice itself; consider how the primary new
offices that Athena promises the Furies concern childbirth and
crop fertility while they also are the ultimate enforcer of the

laws of Athens. Polarity is characteristic of Greek thought, and so Chthonic gods are contrasted with the Olympians who are sky gods, their king being cloud-gathering Zeus. The Olympians are the new, 'progressive' gods who have displaced the elder, 'primitive' Chthonics, a generational dynamic lamented by the Furies throughout *Eumenides*. But polarity is also a form of complementarity, and so, in Burkert's words, 'the opposition between Olympian and Chthonic constitutes a polarity in which one pole cannot exist without the other and in which each pole only receives its full meaning from the other'.[14] Aeschylus' reliance on the pattern of the Hesiodic evolution of the *kosmos* from Gaia, the Earth Goddess, to the Sky God Zeus recurs in this final confrontation between Furies and Zeus' spokesman, Apollo. And yet Aeschylus confuses these polarities by presenting Chthonic goddesses who, when given a chance to speak, talk like the Olympian Athena, and by depicting the supposedly more enlightened Apollo as prone to fits of violent anger and with a certain creative attitude to the truth. By the end of *Eumenides* Apollo will return to his sky home on Olympus and the Furies will descend to their new home in the earth, a polarity balanced in Athena's presence on the earth's surface with her people.

While the Furies appear physically only in *Eumenides*, they have been dynamic forces throughout the *Oresteia*, both named repeatedly and embodied by other agents of rage. The *Oresteia* is largely about the effects of anger, and 'Fury' is the name often given to personify that emotion. Commenting on the tendency of many readers to call the Furies 'primitive', Helen Bacon observes, 'the Furies, who personify this rage, represent a universal psychological reality, not an outmoded "primitive" superstition'.[15] The word 'Erinyes' appears seventeen times in the *Oresteia*: nine times in *Agamemnon* (59, 462, 645, 748, 991, 1119, 1190, 1435, 1579); four in *Libation Bearers* (283, 402, 576, 651); four more in *Eumenides* (331, 344, 512, 950). The closer the Furies are to appearing, the less they are named. Certainly, Aeschylus shows his awareness of how he will denominate the Furies when Cassandra describes the invisible Furies she sees through her prophetic powers as a 'chorus that speaks together but not sounding sweet', the very things they will become visibly in *Eumenides* (*Agamemnon* 1186-7). There are more than twice as many references to Furies in *Agamemnon* than in the other two plays combined, and, even more interestingly, all discussion of Furies stops when Orestes knocks on the palace door (*Libation Bearers* 652). The last word before that knock, *Erinyes*, suggests that he now enacts its spirit, as he intends to kill his mother and her lover. Another 740 lines elapse in the *Oresteia* before anyone says that word again, even though the Pythia, Orestes and Apollo have meanwhile seen the real Furies. Even then, the Furies name themselves three times in their two pretrial songs at Athens before Athena makes an abstract reference to 'a Fury' (950). But she does not name the Furies in front of her, an elision perhaps made more meaningful by the new name she gives them (1041) in the penultimate stanza of the exit song. Once the Furies' threat becomes real, and the Furies are manifest themselves, it seems that their name becomes magically unspeakable.

While the Furies in *Eumenides* seem opposed to the order of Zeus that Apollo represents, the Furies have been acting towards the same purpose as Zeus earlier in the trilogy. Because Zeus sends Agamemnon and Menelaus against Troy as the force of a Fury (*Agamemnon* 40-62, 104-21), some have argued that the Furies are working for Zeus, but this is to overlook the fact that the humans are serving as surrogates of the Furies as restorers of order and justice, not as Furies themselves.[16] At this point the Furies and Zeus pursue parallel actions in enforcing the Fates' unwritten laws. Orestes follows these laws and the commands of Zeus through Apollo in punishing Clytemnestra and Aegisthus, and his actions again are cast throughout *Libation Bearers* as following the force of the Furies, even when he is compelled to choose between his father's Furies and his mother's. Once Clytemnestra is killed the Furies must become their own agents as they lack a human surrogate for the next punishment. In other words, the matricide forces Zeus and the Furies into

divergent paths. Athena's task in *Eumenides*, then, is to restore these parallel paths, or even to make them converge.

Not only do the Chthonic Furies finally emerge as physical
forces in *Eumenides*, but their Olympian opponents do as well.
Neither manifestation is inevitable. Orestes could continue to
be plagued by invisible forces, as at the end of *Libation Bearers*,
and Apollo's priestess, the Pythia, could deliver the god's oracu-
lar word after she emerges from the temple at the beginning of
Eumenides. Instead, the Pythia flees in terror, and Apollo himself instructs Orestes, followed by the first appearance of the
Furies themselves. Apollo's command that Orestes travel to
Athens for Athena's help then requires that she will be manifest
as well.

The play's first setting in Delphi furthers this clash between
Olympian and Chthonic, and between male and female. Delphi
was the centre of the worship of Apollo, the oracle of his father
Zeus, and, although located in a remote, mountainous area, was
one of the most important religious sanctuaries in Greece. The
Pythia's opening speech, which depicts an orderly transition of
Delphic control from Gaia (Earth), to the Titan goddess Themis,
to another Titan Phoebe, and finally to its first male holder
Apollo, contrasts starkly with the more canonical version depicted in the Homeric *Hymn to Apollo*.[17] The earlier hymn tells
the myth of how the young, violent god wanders the countryside
seeking a place for his temple, before stumbling upon the
nymph Telephousa on the slopes of Mt Parnassus. She, reluc-
tant to share the territory, directs him further along to a place
where she knows the she-dragon Typhaon awaits. Apollo
quickly dispatches the she-dragon with his divine, unerring
bow (277-34). In killing this serpent, Apollo re-enacts Zeus'
defeat of the monstrous Typhoeus in Hesiod's *Theogony*, but
both poems play into Apollo's confrontation with the serpentine,
female Furies in *Eumenides*. The bow with which he threatens
the Furies would be a vivid reminder of the hymn's narrative
that the drama's opening seems to suppress. He again will be
the dragon-slayer. Or will he?

The taming, not slaying, of the Furies relies not on Apollo, but on his half-sister Athena in a city whose own myths are full of the conflict between male and female and between Olympian and Chthonic. Its first king Cecrops was half-man, half-snake. Then King Erichthonius was born from the earth when Athena threw on the ground a piece of wool soaked with the semen of Hephaestus, who had suddenly desired her and ejaculated on her leg while in pursuit; this myth is useful to consider when Apollo argues that only fathers have a blood relation to their children (and uses Athena's birth as an example). Another early king, Erechtheus, was told that, if he sacrificed his daughters to the Olympians, Athens would be safe from an imminent invasion. He did so, won the war, but then was destroyed by Poseidon's trident for killing the enemy leader, Eumolpus, a son of Poseidon. His death place on the Acropolis became the location for the temple of Athena Polias, Athena of the City, the very place where the Furies find Orestes when the second part of *Eumenides* begins.

Poseidon and Athena also figure in another Athenian myth that has resonance for the situation and issues of *Eumenides*. During the reign of Cecrops, Athena and Poseidon competed as to which god would receive special offerings from the Athenians and become their principal deity. There are two different versions of what happens next, both relevant to *Eumenides*. In Apollodorus (3.14.1), Poseidon offers a sea to the land of Attica and Athena offers her olive tree.[18] The clash of the two gods becomes so severe that Zeus establishes a tribunal of twelve gods to decide the matter, in an obvious parallel to the Areopagus myth. Athena claims and names Athens after she wins the vote, and Poseidon devastates Attica with floodwaters; note the parallels to the trial and the Furies' threats to Attica. But a version from Varro, preserved in Augustine's *City of God* (18.9), offers a twist on the gender dynamics of *Eumenides*. During Cecrops' rule, both men and women were allowed to vote, and the king had these humans choose between the two gods. The women, who outnumbered men by one, denied Poseidon by a single vote, and, after he devastated Attica, Athens placated him by punishing women in three ways: 'they no longer could cast a vote, no newborn child would take the mother's name, and no one should call the women Athenians'. It is impossible to say with any surety to what extent, if any, these myths played any role in the imagination of Aeschylus and his audience as *Eumenides* was composed and performed, but it is difficult for us to overlook those associations: a shift from a divine to a human group of voters, the victory by a single vote, the removal of authority from women to men, and the victory of Athena, in no small part due to her superior ingenuity.

Athena's very nature suggests she has the means to bring Zeus and the Furies back into accordance with each other. As a goddess of wisdom and the daughter of Mêtis ('Cunning'), she should be able to figure out a way to allow Orestes' acquittal while protecting Athens from the Furies' rage. But her capacity goes far beyond wisdom. Indeed, she and the Furies are in some ways as much alike as Athena and her half-brother Apollo. There are different ways, Hesiodic and Aeschylean in each case, of looking at the parentage of the Furies and Athena. The Aeschylean Furies are solely the daughters of Night and lack a father, but their Hesiodic version has them as the offspring that results from the castration of the first king of the gods, Ouranos (*Theogony* 181-7). Apollo denies the blood relationship of child to mother with the example of Athena's birth from Zeus (*Eumenides* 665-6). I discuss in my detailed account of the play's action how Athena negotiates this claim and then in the chapter on gender and reception its (im)plausibility for the Greeks, but for now I simply observe that Hesiod depicts her as conceived in the womb of Mêtis and then eaten by Zeus so that she is born from his head later (*Theogony* 886-900). Whatever version is in play, the births of Furies and Athena were both unusual and from a single parent. Moreover, both are virgins. Both have strong associations with snakes; the serpent that guarded Athena's treasury on the Acropolis was represented as curled up by her legs in the giant statue inside the Parthenon a few years after the *Oresteia*. This serpentine association further suggests a Chthonic aspect to Athena, and in fact she is believed to have originated as a variation on the earth goddess fertility figure. The source of her name in her city suggests her deep connection to its land, as seen in her promises to the Furies as she tries to dissuade them from blighting the Athenian countryside; they would protect its fertility and receive its first fruits. The Furies represent the rule of the mother, Apollo that of the father. Athena bestrides both worlds, as a protector of the female arts such as weaving and of the male arts of war. Her very androgyny enables her to bridge the divide between Zeus and Furies and transform their earlier parallel efforts into a new structure where Olympian and Chthonic gods will actively cooperate to ensure Justice in the human world. Her lack of commitment to either side in the strife allows her to hand over the decision to a third party. Apollo's protégé becomes safe and the Furies receive the honour they so desperately desire. The court is Athena's innovation, her divine gift to her city, which also provides the Furies with recognition.[19]

In sum, the culmination of Aeschylus' *Eumenides*, if not the entire *Oresteia*, comes not with the institution of the Areopagus tribunal, but with the installation of the Furies in their new home inside the Acropolis after their transformation into the Semnai Theai (or the Eumenides). Greek tragedy itself absorbs and transforms other genres of Greek poetry, including choral lyric and epic. In another type of poem, the hymn, especially in the body of works known as the *Homeric Hymns*, because they are composed in the same style and metre, the dactylic hexameter, as the epics, the singer tells a story that explains how a deity came to have the particular honours and functions that he or she does in the poet's time. In the final responsive songs between Athena and Furies, the dactylic metre suddenly appears. One might say here in conclusion that, by depicting the new honours the Furies receive from Athena and her city, *Eumenides* operates much like a Homeric Hymn. *Eumenides*, especially in its closing songs, is Aeschylus' Hymn to the Eumenides (or Semnai Theai).

3

The Theatre of Aeschylus

The understanding of the theatre in which Aeschylus worked results as much from a close, imaginative reading of his plays as any surviving physical evidence. The attractive ruins of the stone theatre on the south slope of the Acropolis date from the Roman era, several centuries after Aeschylus' death, and that incarnation conceals at least two reconfigurations of the theatrical space. Archaeologists have laboured over the site, but they have reached different conclusions about both the shape and size of the performance space and the area where the spectators sat. In this chapter I shall sketch out the theatre as Aeschylus found it and left it, as well as the context of the performance of the plays in the festival of the City Dionysia. I then close this chapter with an overview of the structural and poetic devices that typified Aeschylean drama in *Eumenides*.[1]

For the sake of clarity, I start by defining a few terms from the Greek theatre, all of which have potentially misleading English derivatives. The *theatron* (seeing place) was the bowl on the south slope of the Acropolis. The *choros* (chorus) was a group of twelve performers who, like the actors, wore masks and had an identity specific to each play. The chorus not only sang, as the name implies to us, but also danced in the *orchêstra*. The *orchêstra* (dancing place) was a circle roughly 25 metres in diameter, in between the *theatron* and the stage.[2] The *skênê* (tent) was a small structure at the back of the *orchêstra*, opposite the *theatron*, which might have had a low platform in front. 'Tent' is somewhat inaccurate, since the presence of actors (usually gods) on top of it indicates a sturdier structure. Its front was probably a canvas panel with a double door.

3. The Theatre of Aeschylus

I now proceed to how the theatre developed before Aeschylus and during his own career.[3] Around 534 BC, Athens established a competition in tragic performances as part of their spring festival the City (or Great) Dionysia, which was held in honour of Dionysus, the Greek god of, among other things, wine and theatre.[4] At the City Dionysia, three playwrights who had been chosen during the previous year by a city magistrate (*archon*) each presented on single days four dramas: three tragedies and a satyr play. These poets competed for prizes and public acclaim. There were also large parades throughout the city, abundant sacrifices of animals, the awarding of public honours in the theatre, and additional competitions involving choruses of fifty men, and others of fifty boys, from the ten tribes of Athens. This festival engaged the entire city as it grew to international significance. Despite the range of activities, the festival's *raison d'être* was the performance of tragedy.

What drove this new institution and its name are equally obscure. The new genre's artists were called *tragoidoi*, 'goat-singers' (perhaps from the prize of a sacrificial goat at the end?), and hence the abstract noun *tragoidia*. While we do not know how and why tragedy began, a plausible scenario and course of events can be hypothesized. Poetry in ancient Greece was always a performative art form, if not necessarily competitive. Bards recite to crowds in Homeric epic and seem sometimes as much concerned about their own glory as that of the heroes whose stories they sing. If tragedy adapted its stories and characters from epic, it took its song and dance from another genre, choral poetry, which was arguably the most important poetic form for Greek society before (and even perhaps after) the growth of tragedy. One particular type of choral poem, the dithyramb, was sung in honour of Dionysus, and the dithyramb, along with tragedy and comedy, was one of the three types of performance at the City Dionysia. Indeed, the close connection between dithyramb and tragedy was emphasized by Aristotle, who claimed that tragedy arose from dithyramb (*Poetics* 1149a14). Herodotus (5.67.5) links this type of song to the development of tragedy (without calling it such) when he ob-

serves that in Sicyon the 'tragic choruses' sung in honour of
Dionysus were transferred to the cult of the hero Adrastus; this
would have occurred late in the sixth century. Around that time
at Corinth Arion was said to develop the dithyramb (Herodotus
1.23), and according to the Byzantine encyclopaedia, the *Suda*,
put on some form of tragedy. But Homer's role here should not
be underestimated. Homeric epic is filled with speeches by its
heroes, and it is not hard to imagine a culture that rewarded
epic performers for especially outstanding embodiments of the
individual characters. It may thus not be a coincidence that
tragedy arose in a city that has also recently instituted tag-
team performances of the complete *Iliad* and *Odyssey* as part of
the Panathenaia, a festival held in honour of the goddess so
complementary to Dionysus, Athena herself.

From 534 BC, when the festival's rules were established and
the tragic genre thus formalized, we have various names of
participants in the City Dionysia, including Aeschylus' immediate predecessor Phrynicus and Thespis, who virtually invented
drama (or at least its prototype), when he stepped forward from
the chorus and, wearing first white lead on his face and later a
mask, personified the hero whose deeds were the subject of the
choral song.[5] These performances were held in the Athenian
Agora, the marketplace and centre of democratic Athens.[6] Since
this space is flat, spectators sat in temporary wooden stands so
that they could see the spectacular dances. The circular dances
of the dithyrambic choruses likely required a corresponding
orchestral shape and needed to be large enough to allow fifty
dancers to move freely. At some point late in the sixth century
the wooden stands collapsed and the decision was made to move
the performances to the sacred precinct of Dionysus on the
south slope of the Acropolis, in order to take advantage of its
natural incline. The precise date of this transfer is uncertain,
and Aeschylus could conceivably have made his debut in 499/8
BC while the Agora was still in use.

The beginning of Aeschylus' career is thus contemporary
with the construction of the Theatre of Dionysus; a timing that
suggests Aeschylus must have played an incalculably large role

in tragedy's early development. It was for good reason that he has been called 'the father of tragedy'. Aristotle's most substantial comments in the *Poetics* about tragedy's evolution concern the changes to the number of actors and the role of the chorus, and both focus on Aeschylus (1449a16): 'Aeschylus was the first to increase the number of its actors from one to two; he reduced the role of the chorus, and made speech play the main role. Sophocles introduced three actors and scenery.'[7] Drama, in the sense of an acted plot that is propelled forwards by conflict, can begin only when a second actor enters the picture, and for 30 to 40 years the Athenian performers of tragedy, following the lead of Thespis, had employed a chorus and a single actor, who sang or chanted responsively to each other. Then, sometime between his debut in 498 and his first surviving drama, *Persians*, Aeschylus began to use a second actor, and tragedy, as we know it, was born.

Aeschylus also almost certainly contributed to the physical development of the Theatre of Dionysus. The new acting area on the south slope of the Acropolis would have retained the large circular *orchêstra*, but now could rely on the natural slope (supplemented by landfill) to contain the spectators. The audience sat on wooden benches, fixed temporarily into the hillside each year for the festival, and this material would have required straight lines gradually angled around the *orchêstra* in the bowl of the *theatron*, a decidedly less compact arrangement than the 'Periclean' version of the 420s, when stone began to be introduced. The early Theatre of Dionysus might thus have seated, officially, as few as 4,000, but as many as the 10,000-15,000 most scholars have believed.[8] Nonetheless, beyond the benches, additional spectators could have sat on the hillside, thus increasing the audience's real size substantially. During Aeschylus' career, the front row of the *theatron* likely ran along roughly one-third of the *orchêstra*'s northern edge and did not engulf two-thirds as it did later. Behind the *orchêstra* the land drops off in elevation into the sanctuary of Dionysus, where a temple to the god is located. With the space more defined than in the Agora, attention could be focused on how actors and chorus enter the acting area, which at this point was only the *orchêstra*; there was no stage, and no *skênê* structure. There were thus two entrance paths, *parodoi*, one to the left and right of the *orchêstra*. Above the eastern entrance, at the edge of the *orchêstra*, there may have been a natural rock outcrop that Aeschylus exploited, especially before the introduction of the *skênê*.[9] From all of these aspects of the early Theatre of Dionysus, it should be clear the focus of the audience was centred on the chorus and actors in the *orchêstra*.

It might seem strange to some that there was no stage and thus no separation between actors and chorus, but this idea of a separation is based upon misunderstanding of Greek performative space. Because the surviving dramas before the *Oresteia* (*Persians, Suppliants* and *Seven against Thebes*) make no reference to any physical structures such as doors or buildings it seems highly unlikely that the *skênê* existed much before the *Oresteia*. The opening lines of *Agamemnon* seem to shout out Aeschylus' enthusiasm for the *skênê*, with the Watchman's clear references to his position on top of the house, followed by Clytemnestra's comings and goings through the palace doors, giving the impression that the poet here is playing with a large new toy and seeing what it can do. The new doors provided a completely different kind of entrance for the actors, who had previously come in along the extended, open-air *parodoi*, thus visible to all well before they first spoke. But the new doors allowed for rapid and surprise entrances, as seen throughout the *Oresteia*, especially in the second and third plays.

The *skênê* allowed for and brought about other changes. The sheer size of the *theatron* may have quickly led to the realization that actors needed some kind of sounding board to project their voices, and the wooden and canvas *skênê*, accompanied perhaps by a low wooden platform, would have served nicely.[10] Changes to the actors' masks may have also helped actors make their voices seem louder (though this is not to be confused with the late use of small megaphones in masks). Aeschylus, who acted in all of his plays, must have been quite aware of what means increased the effectiveness of his art, and doubtless

38

experimented constantly. The ancient *Life* (14) records that Aeschylus 'organized the *skênê*', which suggests that this experiment at least was successful. Most scholars believe that, even if there was a stage, it would have been low enough to allow actors – and, in the case of *Eumenides*, the chorus as well – to move easily onto the floor of the *orchêstra*. That the *orchêstra* remains the primary acting area for the *Oresteia* can be shown if one tries to construct the trial of Orestes on a stage small enough so that it does not overwhelm the *orchêstra*.

The creation of an interior, hidden space inside the *skênê* afforded the dramatists new opportunities to expand the action's spatial dynamics, and here again Aeschylus the innovator, if not inventor, was at work. Aeschylus, while composing a set of dramas about what happens inside a particular house, was intrigued by the symbolic possibilities of the tension between inside and outside, between open and hidden, between female interior and male exterior. He thus was challenged to find a way to bring these spaces into stark contrast with great speed, often in the process collapsing these distinctions.

The way he found was probably a device called the *ekkyklêma*, literally, 'the wheeled out thing', which was a small wooden wheeled platform that could be moved quickly through the double doors of the *skênê*. Based on its probable use in the *Oresteia*, it had to be at least large enough to hold two prone bodies and one standing actor.[11] The most recent scholar (and accomplished theatre practitioner) to weigh in on this topic, Graham Ley, has suggested that some of the uncertainties surrounding textual indications of the *ekkyklêma* may be resolved by considering the innovative Aeschylus' excitement at suddenly possessing a new tool while working on the *Oresteia*, as Aeschylus especially revised the *Eumenides* to incorporate its use.[12] Ley's suggestion is, of course, speculative, but it agrees with the larger picture of an Aeschylus who was as much a creature of the theatre as he was a great poet. And his theatre, which both accompanied and caused the growth of Athenian theatrical practice as a whole, was by necessity innovative and original. With the theatre before and

39

of Aeschylus established, let us look briefly at the workings of his *Eumenides*.

The theatre of Aeschylus' *Eumenides*

Let us summarize the physical, inanimate aspects of Aeschylean theatre before turning to the people who inhabited the space. A round *orchêstra*, roughly 25 metres in diameter, lay at the bottom of a natural slope, which was hollowed out to form a bowl where the spectators sat. At the eastern side of the *orchêstra* there may have been a natural rock outcropping (*pagos*) to which Athena points when she refers to the Areopagus as the 'this rock (*pagos*) of Ares'.[13] At the opposite side of the *orchêstra* from the *theatron* stood a small building with double doors, which may or may not have had a low stage in front. Performers could enter the acting area through these doors, above the *skênê*, or along one of the open entrances at either side of the *orchêstra*. The acting area was relatively uncluttered, occupied only by props and objects necessary to indicate the play's locale.

The *skênê* of *Eumenides* unusually represents two completely different cities, and two different locales in the same city, and, as the action moves from one to the other, the *skênê* become less important. The *skênê* retains the large double doors of the first two plays, but here they mark the entrances to two temples, first Apollo's at Delphi and then Athena's at Athens, and not the entrance to the palace of a dynastic, troubled clan. I often wonder to what extent the Delphic *skênê* front would have retained the turbulent, bloody associations of the first two plays since its basic appearance was the same, and, when the action begins, the events resemble what has preceded them. The *skênê* doors still conceal something troubling, violent, and monstrous. Moreover, in *Agamemnon* the statue of Apollo Agyiates, 'Apollo of the Street', at the entrance to Agamemnon's palace, combined with the cries of Cassandra to Apollo who has led her here, as a bride, to this house, earlier marked the *skênê* of *Agamemnon* as belonging to Apollo as well. The house has thus moved from being metaphorically to literally Apollo's.[14] In other words, the

40

'scene' has changed, but the *skênê*, and what it has represented, remains the same. As the action shifts from Delphi to Athens, the focus shifts from the *skênê* to the *orchêstra*, from what the palace has represented to the characters themselves. From the house, to the civic collective.

Who were the performers in this symbolic spatial shift? The most important component of the performers was not the actors, but the chorus, without which no Greek would have recognized a performance of tragedy as legitimate. Tragedy grew out of choral performance and the physical reality of the choral unit, dominating the acting area, never really diminished, even if its role in the plot was reduced as it moved from Aeschylus' hands to Euripides'. Moreover, when a tragic poet applied to the archon for permission to compete in the Dionysia, he did not request actors, but that he be 'granted a chorus'. Financed by a wealthy Athenian, twelve skilled dancers and singers (later increased by Sophocles to fifteen) would train throughout the year for the parts in the four plays that would be staged consecutively in a single day.[15] Participation in a chorus thus required a good singing voice, dance skills and a fair amount of stamina. And, considering that the same dozen performers had to impersonate, in a single day, grumpy old men, angry slave women, even angrier Furies, and then a collection of tipsy, randy satyrs, a certain amount of acting ability must have been required.

The actors required similar stamina, skills and expressive range. Only three actors were allowed to each poet. Masks allowed each actor to play multiple parts. The so-called 'Rule of the Three Actors' was probably established in order to create a level playing field, and it should be thus seen as 'an opportunity for the playwrights rather than as a straightjacket'.[16] In the *Oresteia*, perhaps for the first time, Aeschylus employs three actors, and, in the trial scene of *Eumenides*, begins to use three actors speaking throughout a single scene. One of the three must have played only Orestes, since Orestes has a prominent role in every scene. The second may have played the three females: the Pythia, Clytemnestra and Athena. The third, who was likely, due to the role's size, to have been the weakest actor, could have played only Apollo. On the other hand, the same actor could have played Apollo and the Pythia, especially given the size of Athena's part. Aeschylus, who performed in his own works, would have needed to hire only two additional actors. The trilogic *Oresteia* presents the complex problem of trying to decide which parts Aeschylus would have chosen for himself, and which parts the other actors received. Did the same actor play Clytemnestra in all three? If Aeschylus (or whoever was the most talented actor) took the biggest part each time, he would have moved from Clytemnestra in *Agamemnon* to Orestes in *Eumenides*. Or is Athena the most important part? If Electra is the emotional centre of *Libation Bearers*, then perhaps Aeschylus' thespian specialty was female parts. C.W. Marshall, who has exhaustively studied all the suggestions for part distribution in the *Oresteia* (neatly summarized in a table[17]), indeed suggests that the same actor in all three plays, who then also took the part of Athena in *Eumenides*, played Clytemnestra. Given the complementarity of the androgynous, malevolently persuasive Clytemnestra of *Agamemnon* and the androgynous, beneficently persuasive Athena, it is very suggestive that they would have been embodied by the same performer. Beyond the three actors and chorus, *Eumenides* in its last scene requires an unusual number of extra performers. These include a herald and trumpeter who signal the trial's inception, the ten or eleven Athenian citizens who compose the Areopagite jury, finally accompanied by the attendants and priestess of Athena Polias.

The costumes these actors wore form part of the playwright's means to signal the conflict of *Eumenides* and its resolution. The Pythia, despite her age, was dressed in the white robe of a maiden girl, suggesting her purity,[18] and Orestes wears a white suppliant's wreath (45), offset by the red blood on his sword. There is no reference to Apollo's clothing, yet traditional iconography invariably represents him with pure white vestments, and, since Aeschylus needs him to be instantly recognizable, he must have appeared in this way, accompanied by his lethal bow. This whiteness contrasts with the black robes and masks (lines

52, 55) of the Furies. The blood on Orestes' sword is next matched by the bloodstains on Clytemnestra's clothing, the same she wore in the previous play, stains that she shows the Furies. The reddish purple of these blood marks are then transformed into the purple robes that the Furies don (1028) when they become the Eumenides, divine protectors of Athens. The dark Furies' robes would further contrast with the gleaming bronze of Athena's armour. The Furies' masks likely resembled the heads of Gorgons.[19] Last, the shift from the heroic world to modern Athens would be signalled by the presence of the Areopagites, who were doubtless clothed like the normal Athenian citizens of the audience, and the attendants and priestess of the temple of Athena Polias, who must have been adorned in a way that immediately signalled their identities; perhaps they even appear as their real counterparts did when they paraded in the Panathenaic procession, one of the central civic events of Athens. Thus the costumes, and their colours in particular, are an important part of the visual vocabulary of *Eumenides* and contribute to its meaning.

The audience of *Eumenides* would have expected a structural rhythm, alternating between choral singing and speech by actors. They would have expected the chorus to march all together into and out of the *orchêstra* to a specific metre, the anapaest; but, as we shall see, Aeschylus violates this practice in *Eumenides* in a way that suggests the turmoil caused by Orestes' murder of his mother. The Furies have difficulty behaving and performing like a normal chorus until the end, when they are joined in their singing by Athena, and by a second chorus of Athenian women, all signifying the new harmony achieved in the course of the play.

4

The Play and its Staging

As the *Eumenides* begins, the audience has already watched the
Oresteia's first two parts. Aeschylus has trained his audience
through the first two plays to watch for certain themes and
patterns of action that are embodied in the actors and staging.
Each has ended with a double murder, an attempt by their
agent to justify the bloodshed, and the further destruction of the
stage community by a police squad invading the acting area; in
Agamemnon, the bodyguard of the cowardly usurper Aegisthus
forces the chorus of Argive elders into submission, and in
Libation Bearers the Furies, seen only by Orestes, pursue him
from the stage and out of Argos. The hopes of first the Watchman and then Orestes himself that the House of Atreus might
find release from its turmoils have been dashed. In this chapter
I shall address what happens during *Eumenides* and how it
happens, for the dramaturgy of the play is quite remarkable;
moreover, more uncertainty and controversy surround the staging of *Eumenides* than that of virtually any other extant Greek
tragic drama. *Eumenides*, especially compared to its two predecessors, is a brief play, but even so it presents scenes of great
speed and variety in ways that often confound expectation and
heighten suspense.

After a short break so that the audience can catch its breath
and satisfy various bodily needs (it is, after all, a long day at the
theatre!), the action starts anew, for the first time outside
Argos, at Delphi, the seat of Apollo's ancient oracle. While
Agamemnon had evoked the wider world of the Trojan War, its
concerns were narrowly focused on Argos and its royal house,
whose double doors concealed the House of Atreus' bloody past

and marked the border between the public and private, male and female, known and secret. *Libation Bearers* felt claustrophobic with its suffocating concentration on Agamemnon's tomb and the house's doorway. *Eumenides* hugely expands this world to encompass, unexpectedly, not one but two other places: first Delphi, then Athens. The poet thus needs to mark this transformation. During the break, stage hands have removed whatever props marked the acting area as the palace of Agamemnon at Argos and have now added some tokens to signal that the *skênê* now is the Temple of Apollo at Delphi; perhaps Aeschylus used large tripods such as traditionally stood outside this temple or perhaps he simply relied on the first words of the priestess, which leave little doubt as to the scene. Nonetheless, the large palace doors remain in place, now serving as the temple doors, and the events of the first two parts of the trilogy have alerted the audience to pay close attention to what happens when characters enter and exit there.

In the following discussion I give entrance and exit directions from the perspective of the audience, not of the actors. Most scholars of Greek theatre now accept that the right was used for entrances to and from the setting's city, the left for entrances from the rest of the world and from nature.[1] Thus, in the first part of *Eumenides* the Pythia enters from Delphi on the right, but in the second part, Orestes enters from Delphi on the left, since the right is now Athens.

Prologue and scene 1: (a) 1-93

Eumenides is remarkably free in its form, especially at its opening, which lacks the typical solo speech or dialogue followed by the choral entry song (*parodos*). Instead, Aeschylus here presents a fairly rapid sequence of three smaller exchanges among characters and chorus that culminates in Apollo's violent confrontation with the chorus of Furies, who, meanwhile, have made a most unusual entrance. But this is not a typical chorus.

Despite this relative singularity, the opening of *Eumenides* restates the pattern introduced in *Agamemnon* and continued in *Libation Bearers*: a human character establishes the play's setting and tone and then witnesses an event that runs against the character's expectations, thus launching the drama's action. Here the character is the elderly Pythia, the priestess of Apollo at Delphi, who serves as the speaker of the prophecies the god himself delivers to her. This female is the second priestess of Apollo the audience has met, and Aeschylus signals the coming resolution of the trilogy's crises by presenting this second prophetess as an unproblematic, recognizably traditional figure, and not the crazed, impassioned, would-be lover of the god himself, Cassandra. The audience members have no personal experience with cursed Trojan princesses, but the Pythia is certainly a figure they themselves or acquaintances could have encountered during trips to Delphi. Though certainly on a more exalted level, the Pythia thus belongs to the world of the Watchman and the Herald in *Agamemnon* and the Nurse in *Libation Bearers*.

The Pythia enters from the right wing (again, audience's right), praying to the gods of Delphi, and offering sacrifice – perhaps at an altar in the centre of the *orchestra* – as if it were any normal day. Little does she know what lurks inside the god's temple. Her speech narrates the mythical history of Delphi, with Chthonic goddesses peacefully relinquishing control of Delphi to the Olympians, a history which mirrors the trilogy's larger movements, as first Gaia the Earth Mother ruled Delphi, then Gaia's daughter the Titan Themis, then the goddess Phoebe, who finally handed it over to the Olympian Apollo, who thus became Delphi's first male occupant. Just as Aeschylus had earlier altered the Homeric account of Agamemnon's death to stress Clytemnestra's role, so too here he meaningfully transforms an established traditional account, found in the Homeric *Hymn to Apollo*, that represented Delphi founding as an act of civilizing violence by the male over its primitive female inhabitants. In her remembrance of the Bacchic maenads' pursuit of Pentheus, who was, like Orestes, a late-adolescent male (*ephebe*) with a complex relationship with his mother, the

Pythia foreshadows the gendered conflicts between the Furies and Apollo and, in her closing prayer to Athena (201), the trial of Orestes under the goddess's watch, as well as the pursuit of Orestes by the Furies (24-6). Unlike Orestes, Pentheus lost his maternal struggle and found his crazed mother Agave ripping his head off in the belief he was a lion, as dramatized in a trilogy (now lost) by Aeschylus himself and fifty years later by Euripides in his *Bacchae*. The Furies' later description of themselves as 'mortal-watching maenads' (499-500) strengthens the connection between these two mythic scenarios. The allusion to the myth of Pentheus and the Bacchants thus suggests the danger of the mother, yet also establishes the pattern that Orestes will reverse. Despite the ominous background to this allusion, the general effect of the Pythia's speech is orderly, but the Furies' emergence will shatter this image in a few moments.

As the final part of the Pythia's prayers that open the religious business of the temple for the day, she makes an offering to her imagined audience that might slip by unnoticed by us, but which might be important for understanding how Aeschylus meaningfully involves the theatre audience in the action once the scene shifts to Athens (31-2): 'If there are some people from the Greeks present, let them draw lots and then enter, as is custom.' Historically, each day it was open, a throng gathered outside the Temple of Apollo for answers to questions both great and small. Many Athenians at the time of the *Oresteia*'s production would have personal knowledge of these matters, and the audience might thus feel they themselves are waiting their turn.[2] Aeschylus thus makes the audience feel it is part of the ritual life of Delphi, just as he will later involve the audience in the trial at Athens. Her prayers completed, the Pythia enters Apollo's temple. Since Orestes had announced at the end of *Libation Bearers* that he would journey to Delphi for purification and protection by Apollo and then ran from the stage pursued by the invisible mob of the Furies, the audience must suspect what the Pythia will find, but it must also be in doubt whether what she sees in there will be visible to them, since only Orestes saw the Furies at the end of *Libation Bearers*.

47

Perhaps the audience expects Orestes to appear from the temple doors next.

The Pythia's entrance into the temple destroys this reverent meditation, for, as with the first two dramas, passages through the doors are fraught with tension and danger. The acting area is momentarily, and atypically, empty, and then, after a brief pause, the Pythia reappears in a manner utterly unlike her entrance into the temple: scurrying on all fours like an animal, in a blind panic at what she has seen. Clearly, the Furies are no longer invisible to all save Orestes. Since the gods, including the Furies, have been unseen yet named forces throughout the *Oresteia*, the audience has little reason to expect their embodiment. Aeschylus carefully here builds the audience's anticipation first by withholding the initial appearance of the Furies and then by having the Pythia describe the horrific scene she has seen inside the temple before the audience is allowed access to that vision. According to the Pythia, Orestes sits at the *omphalos* stone, the navel stone, a sacred object believed to be the rock Kronos ate instead of the infant Zeus; Kronos had been swallowing his children out of a fear they would overthrow him. This episode forms part of the three-stage 'Succession Myth' evoked in the Hymn to Zeus in *Agamemnon* (167-72), and the *omphalos* stone thus recalls that earlier recounting of a divine progression that implied hope for an analogous improvement among humans. The stone allowed Zeus' mother Rhea to hide him from his murderous father (Hesiod, *Theogony* 459-506), and so, like Orestes' murder of his mother, which relied on a false tale of his own death, deception enabled Zeus' rise against the older order. Placed next to the Temple of Apollo at Delphi, the stone was the centre of the world according to Greek religion. Orestes crouches there in supplication, a posture that provides him with divine protection. He holds in one hand a suppliant branch of laurel bound with fillets of wool, and in the other a sword still dripping with his mother Clytemnestra's blood. The Furies, whom the Pythia does not know and thus does not name, surround him. The Furies are dressed in black, with snakes visible in their hair and clothing. The Pythia does not mention Apollo's presence at all, and merely prays that he come to sort out this crisis. She exits the acting area, likely via the same path she used for her arrival, but now with an entirely different, much more Cassandra-like, deportment. The acting area is again, momentarily, empty. More suspense. The eyes of the audience members must surely be drawn to the doors.

Once again in the *Oresteia*, the *skênê*'s double doors become centrally important, and in a way that could suggest the corpse-filled tableaux in the final scenes of its first two parts. The doors open, and suddenly Orestes, Apollo, and, at some point, the Furies appear, and so the Olympian gods, evoked in prayer and acting mysteriously behind the scenes throughout the *Oresteia*'s earlier episodes, have unexpectedly now become manifest agents in the action, joined by the Chthonic Furies, themselves previously invisible. Matricide has provoked such a crisis that gods will now enter into conflict as visible agents with other gods. Because the Pythia's vision has upset her so much and because the relation between gods and men is so central to this play, it is important to consider what the audience probably now saw. The surviving manuscripts from late antiquity do not contain any stage directions, and thus, when there are no clear textual signals of what characters are doing and how they are doing it, we must fall back on the texts and on what meagre evidence exists about ancient theatre practice. Scholars disagree sharply about Apollo's location relative to Orestes and how visible Orestes and the Furies are initially. If Aeschylus did not make use of the *ekkyklêma*, then Apollo and Orestes walk out of the temple doors and the Furies remain completely invisible to the audience for a few minutes longer.[3] Or the Pythia's departure is followed by the doors opening and the *ekkyklêma* being rolled out to display the precise scene that she had described: Orestes, sitting next to the navel stone, with at least three Furies (140) visible in front, asleep, so that their robes are apparent but their horrifying visages are not.[4] In the temple's inner recesses the other nine Furies lurk out of view, emerging only when the first three move into action and clear the entrance. One argument against the use of the *ekkyklêma* here, that one that could hold several sleeping Furies and Orestes with the navel-stone (and possibly even Apollo) would be impracticably large, is answered by the Pythia's reference (47) to the Furies asleep 'on chairs', a position that certainly sounds uncomfortable but is dramaturgically convenient in occupying far less space than would prone bodies.⁵

The Furies thus are here menacingly present, yet have not yet entered, situated as they are liminally between temple interior and acting area, and Orestes desperately awaits Apollo's arrival, which finally takes place after a brief pause so that the audience can take in the scenario. The full impact of the Furies' horror awaits the actors' departure, when the nine hidden chorus members spill out of the entrance to join the initial three. The bloody sword in Orestes' hand and the motionless bodies of Orestes and the Furies in the temple's doorway must evoke the earlier scenes of first Clytemnestra and then Orestes standing over their victims, but this time the authority figure who seizes control of this portal will be divine.

Suddenly Apollo, the subject of Cassandra's laments in *Agamemnon* and Orestes' unseen instigator in *Libation Bearers*, appears, either from inside the temple's dark recesses at the back of the *ekkyklêma* or authoritatively above the temple on the *skênê* roof, protecting yet physically remote from Orestes.⁶ Presumably Apollo bears his bow, thus implying the threat of violence against the Furies. The Olympians are finally present and communicating directly with humans, who are no longer left to their own devices. Apollo's promise to Orestes, that he will receive a 'release from his toils' in Athens (83), answers in identical language the Watchman's first prayer in *Agamemnon*.

Apollo repeats his promise of protection, instructs Orestes to travel to Athens and supplicate Athena's statue on the Acropolis, and offers him the further guidance of Apollo's brother Hermes, protector of travellers. While some commentators have suggested that a silent actor who plays Hermes accompanies Orestes, others now believe this is unnecessary.⁷ Yet *Eumenides* is characterized by a visible embodiment of the invisible divine forces evoked and sensed through the *Oresteia*'s

first two plays, and 'Hermes' is the first word of *Libation
Bearers* in Orestes' prayer at his father's tomb. More problematic is Apollo's inability to resolve Orestes' dilemma personally;
even his confession that he will send Orestes to Athena because
'I persuaded you to kill your mother' (84) rings somewhat hollow
because Orestes (and the audience) heard much more in the
way of threats to Orestes in *Libation Bearers* (269-97, 1029-33)
than the sort of persuasion Athena will bring to bear on the
angry Furies. And it is very unclear whether Apollo intimates
exactly what Athena will do to help Orestes, since, while Apollo
mentions jurors and words to charm them (81-2), his prophetic
vision seems cloudy and imprecise. Apollo's own spotty performance in the trial suggests he does not have this procedure fully
understood or under tight control. Orestes exits one way to the
left, Apollo another (into his temple), and the acting area empties, momentarily, for a third time. More suspense. What about
the Furies? When will the chorus enter?

Prologue and scene 1 (b): 94-298

While expectations continue that the chorus will finally begin
its first song and dance, Aeschylus instead quickly introduces
yet another character, the fourth, the ghost of Clytemnestra,
whose renewed cries to the Furies balance and respond to
Orestes' urgent appeals to his own champion Apollo. We can
only speculate how Aeschylus staged her arrival, but there are
three possibilities. She could have walked in through one of the
side entrances, an attractive idea if we take literally her complaint (98), 'I wander shamefully'. Or she could have appeared
from inside the temple. Or, representing an ascent from the
Underworld, she could have emerged through a trap door in the
low wooden platform in front of the *skênê*; this would afford the
actor, if some of the Furies are visibly asleep on the *ekkyklêma*,
the opportunity to chastise them in close physical proximity (a
reasonably natural staging). Last, she could have entered from
behind or from a whole in the rock outcrop in the eastern edge
of the *orchêstra*, near the stage; if so, then her elevated position

could respond to Apollo's appearance on the temple roof, if indeed he was there and if there was a rock (so many 'ifs' in these staging matters!). The Chthonic Clytemnestra would thus emerge from below to answer the sky god Olympian Apollo, if his first entrance was on the *skênê* roof, or Apollo himself then balances the hilltop Clytemnestra by denouncing the Furies from above the temple. Now, regardless of its manner, it is indeed an angry arrival. Just as the living Clytemnestra resented her marginalization and lack of honour as a woman, so too now the dead one is bitter about her place among the dead. Showing her wounds to the Furies, she demands vengeance, and lacking a mortal or Olympian avenger, she requires the Furies to act on her behalf. Casting Orestes as a fawn pursued by the hound-like Furies (111), Clytemnestra here reactivates one of the trilogy's dominant metaphors, the hunt, which the Furies then develop through their first songs.[8] From the opening lines of *Agamemnon*, with its insomniac Watchman, sleeping and wakefulness have also been key themes, which become newly urgent now. With the Furies awake and again on the trail, Clytemnestra, for the final time, withdraws (back through the trap door, back up the entrance path, back into the temple, or back into or behind the rock). Once again, no actors are visible and the Furies have the opportunity to take over, literally, the acting area. The action now moves towards the confrontation of Furies and Apollo.

After a series of moaning, inarticulate cries as Clytemnestra ceases to goad their sleep, the Furies finally enter, though, as has happened so often already in this play, in a violation of typical Athenian theatrical practice, where the unified choral movements tended to represent some form of stable corporate entity, often a collective that embodied the *polis* community. The Furies, of course, with their insistence on blood vengeance, are antithetical to the legal mechanisms on which the *polis* is predicated and for which Orestes' trial provides a charter myth. It is difficult to overstress the remarkable nature of the chorus' entrance after its leader arises from sleep and turns to waken two of her comrades (140-2); as they arise, the full horror of their appearance is made manifest to the audience, a horror which grows as the other nine follow. They begin a song of iambics mixed with dochmaics, the latter metre typically indicating extreme agitation and emotion. This is the oddest choral entrance in all of the surviving works of Greek tragedy. As William Scott observes, 'members of the chorus awaken to find themselves already onstage and the play so far under way that they must run to catch it'.[9] Whether or not the Furies first appear on the *ekkyklêma*, the main impact of their entrance remains the same: instead of a unanimous entrance from one of the side wings, the Furies spill out, one by one, or in small groups, and through the *skênê* door.[10] Further, they sing (and moan and shriek) often individually, not as a group. The effect is one of anarchy. The first song continues the theme of the hunt, and introduces the inter-generational divine conflict that will dominate most of this drama, as they lament *hoi neôteroi theoi*, the new/young gods who disrespect *dikê*, justice (162).

Having delayed the Furies' entrance for as long as possible and associated them with the disruption of musical and theatrical conventions, Aeschylus now brings them into direct conflict with the Olympian god who stands as the very antithesis of their loathsome appearance and chaos: Apollo, the god of order. The image of Apollo, the handsome, eternally youthful late adolescent male, contrasts starkly with the aged, dark, hideous beings who swarm around his temple.

While the Furies criticize Apollo's behaviour, the Delphic god in turn (178) assaults their very existence and appearance in a series of extraordinarily vehement insults. It is unclear, because of the speed of his unannounced entrance, whether he emerges from the temple behind them or suddenly stands above it. But since the Furies are willingly departing the temple in search of the fugitive Orestes, Apollo's stern commands, 'Get out of my house, quickly, I order' (179-80), seem unnecessary and perhaps in false bravado. And yet, because Apollo threatens them with violence from his divine bow and inescapable arrows (181), there seems at first little hope that this confrontation will be resolved peacefully. However, Apollo's choice of violent words, not actions, in attempting to resolve this crisis itself prepares for Athena's later more successful, and more earnest, persuasion of the Furies to accept the trial's outcome and their new role in Athens. Again, because of the Furies' strong associations with snakes from the moment Orestes and the Pythia first see them (*Libation Bearers* 1017, 1050; *Eumenides* 128), here it would be difficult to escape reminders of Apollo's first conquest of Delphi, as depicted in the Homeric *Hymn to Apollo*, with this very same weaponry.[11] While the Furies' first song has questioned Apollo's behaviour in helping a matricide escape, undermining justice and polluting his own temple, Apollo's response centres on his capacity to inflict pain on their bodies, the appearance of which he denounces in great detail. The Furies defy expectation by not reciprocating, but responding with calm, reasonable questions that focus on the justifications for matricide; even their initial address, 'Lord Apollo', is surprisingly respectful. This exchange, which allows the Furies to assert the primacy of pursuing matricides (210), foreshadows the debate in Orestes' trial, yet still shows the trial's necessity because the two sides argue to a standstill. Apollo senses an inconsistency in the Furies' insistence on punishing only one kind of murder (of blood kin), just as Clytemnestra had angrily denounced the Argive elders, who raged against her for killing Agamemnon, for threatening her with banishment after they had not punished Agamemnon for the murder of Iphigenia (*Agamemnon* 1412-22). What is needed, and what the later trial will offer, is some kind of consistent justice. Apollo further asserts that the Furies dishonour the marriage of Zeus and Hera by ignoring the murder of a husband by his wife (213-16). The Furies continue to argue in the name of justice (230), while Apollo skirts that concept and stresses instead Orestes' sacred status as a suppliant who must be protected (205, 233-4).[12] The first dispute ends in stalemate, and Apollo tells the Furies of his plans for Athena to adjudicate Orestes' case (224).

Apollo vanishes into his temple, and the Furies exit, through the left wing, in pursuit of Orestes before he reaches Athens.

Apollo cannot stop them, just as they cannot break the physical supplication of Orestes first with the navel stone and second, in the next scene, with the statue of Athena (another stalemate). Again, the acting area empties.

Scene 2: 235-320

At this point both time and space become fluid, extraordinarily so for Greek tragedy, which normally engages its action in a fairly compressed period and in a single place. The unnatural speed of the passage of the signal fires from Troy to Argos in *Agamemnon* does not typify drama's handling of time, but it does prepare for this much freer setting. A substantial, though indeterminate, amount of time elapses in between Orestes' flight and his arrival in Athens, as Orestes' *miasma* (pollution from the shedding of kindred blood) has been worn away by his long wanderings and purification rituals at the houses of other men. If Aeschylus had placed visible tokens of Delphi, such as tripods, at the drama's beginning, then these would have been removed, leaving a blanker canvas for the poet's words and the audience's imagination, though stage hands at that moment might have carried in the statue of Athena (unless the Pythia's reference to Athena Pronaia, 'Athena before the temple', at line 21 indicates a statue in the Delphi setting).[13] The exact locale of the action at this point, other than 'somewhere in Athens', is somewhat vague, since clearly that later trial (566) occurs at the Areopagus, but Orestes on his arrival claims suppliant status at a temple of Athena, which did not exist on the Areopagus. Apollo has instructed Orestes to seek in Athens the 'ancient statue' of Athena, language that suggests the icon of Athena Polias, 'Athena of the City', whose temple stood on the Acropolis. Presumably, Aeschylus leaves this space undefined in order to enable the quick shift to the trial, which cannot happen anywhere other than at the Areopagus.

The setting's physical appearance here marks a momentous shift in the *Oresteia*, since, for the first time, the large double doors in the *skênê* no longer factor in the drama's action and themes. The final exit from those doors was the Furies' entrance into the acting area, and, if Apollo's confrontation with the Furies takes place with him in the *orchêstra* and not atop the shed, then his departure into them at 234 is the last use of doors in the *Oresteia*.[14] The doors had marked the violent past of the House of Atreus, and the inner mysteries of the Temple of Apollo. Indeed, those doors *were* the House of Atreus itself. The House and its concerns thus fade away, literally and figuratively, replaced by the Athenian *polis*. There are no more mysteries, no more dark secrets hidden away, and all is out in the open. The reconfiguration of the *Oresteia*'s dramatic space thus mirrors its thematic progress.[15]

And yet a new scene has started, without the intervention of the requisite choral song. The main structural dynamic of Greek drama is an alternation between choral songs and dialogue,[16] and it should already be apparent that *Eumenides* does not really conform to this pattern. The choral entry song should follow an initial speech or dialogue, and the chorus should then remain until the drama's end, with their songs framing the episodes. The rare instances where the chorus leaves and returns in the drama's middle, such as Sophocles' *Ajax* (814, 866) and Euripides' *Alcestis* (746, 872), mark a major shift in the direction of the drama's action, a kind of second start. As the previous scene in *Eumenides* ended, the chorus exited, and then Apollo, leaving the acting area bare, thus signalling that the action is about to begin anew. The scene shifts now to Athens, yet, just as an actor, not the chorus, had initiated the first movement, so too now does the second begin not with an intermediary choral song, but with an actor's speech. While it is possible that the removal of the chorus and Orestes' next words suffice to change the scene, it seems more likely (to me, at least) that stage hands have signalled the rare scene change by removing whatever visible means Aeschylus used to signify Delphi and then carrying a statue of Athena to an area in the orchestra relatively near the *skênê*, so that, after Orestes enters from the left, he falls at the foot of this statue in supplication, an image that would echo his first appearance when he was clinging to the navel-stone at Delphi. However, the *ekkyklêma* possibly brought out the statue of Athena, which, since the image of Orestes clutching it would evoke Orestes and the navel-stone in the first scene, would visually strengthen the parallel between the two supplications; such a location, however, would then make it impossible for the Furies to dance around Orestes.[17] The Furies arrive, also from the left, hotly pursuing their victim. Unlike Orestes' first appearance as a suppliant, surrounded by sleeping Furies, his antagonists are awake. Finally, Clytemnestra's hounds and their prey stand face to face.

Orestes' first speech and his initial exchange with the Furies both focus on his peculiar ritual status. The Furies have been able to track Orestes, like hounds, because they can smell his mother's blood on his hands. The Greeks believed that bloodshed, especially kindred, left a stain of pollution (*miasma*) on its perpetrator, but also that the good blood shed in animal sacrifice could cleanse this bad blood. The preferred method of sacrificial purification, which Orestes experiences (280-3), involved cutting a pig's throat over the polluted person's head to wash his head and hands with blood.[18] As Burkert observes, purification by blood is a rite of passage, as the murderer is reincorporated into the community, but a swine head's close associations with the female genitalia lend this event associations of rebirth. As Orestes at Delphi, near the navel-stone, is bathed in sacrificial blood, he is reborn, and the sense that he is Clytemnestra's son is eroded even further, thus preparing for Apollo's argument during the trial that denies the mother's role in the son's birth.[19] In a sense he becomes Apollo's son more than Clytemnestra's. Indeed, in vase paintings that show Apollo and Orestes together (fending off the Furies), they appear almost indistinguishable as handsome, aristocratic males in late adolescence. Orestes himself suggests this distancing from the maternal in specifying that the swine blood has purified 'mother-killing *miasma*'.

Orestes' first and second speeches to Athena's statue stress that his guilt has been 'worn away at shrines', that he comes with his hand 'not uncleansed' (237-9). But that Apollo's ritual purifications at Delphi have failed, at least as far as the Furies are concerned, is signalled by Aeschylus' term for a lack of purification, *aphoibanton*, which puns on Apollo's epithet Phoebus (*Phoibos*). However, clearly in the eyes of all but the Furies he has been cleansed by Apollo, through the blood ordeal of his fugitive exile, and by repeated rituals at the homes he has visited during his travel. Orestes thus is purified and Athena recognizes that he is ritually clean under normal circumstances (474), but being a matricide is certainly no normal circumstance and thus further, more extraordinary steps are required; the legal remedy becomes necessary because the ritual is not efficacious.[20] Orestes prays to Athena, but prayers to the Olympian gods in the *Oresteia* appear to have failed at every utterance. Despite Apollo's assurances (and the audience would have cause, based on what they have seen and heard during the performance, to doubt his credibility), Athena's arrival seems in doubt. At the very least, she may arrive too late, after the Furies have caught up with Orestes.

The urgent singularity of Orestes' situation continues to be matched by the singularity of the poetic form of *Eumenides*. Scene changes in Greek tragedy are rare enough, but the break here with no choral interlude is completely unique. Instead, the chorus sings following Orestes' prayer to Athena. While the text lacks signals as to the manner of the second entrance of the Furies, it seems very possible, if not likely, that they would hurry into the *orchêstra* not as a group but sporadically, just as they first entered through the temple door, an entrance which, combined with the image of the second supplication of Orestes, would create a compelling mirror scene. The choral singing, which should have occurred before Orestes' prayer, now is after it and very brief (254-75), suggesting they barely have time to sing, so relentless is their pursuit, and lines 254-63 seem spoken by individual chorus members. Even the metres Aeschylus uses for this song, combined with its formlessness, reinforce the sense of anarchic speed and confusion.[21] For the first time the audience hears what awaits Orestes if Furies lay hold of him:

they will drink his blood (264-6), and he will serve as a sacrificial feast for them, but eaten alive, not first sacrificed at an altar (305). Orestes would thus be the last of the many perverted sacrifices in the *Oresteia*, most notably echoing his sister Iphigenia.[22] And to bring him to their desires, the Furies use, like the other gods in *Eumenides*, not force but words: their Binding Song. And with this song, the Furies finally begin to order themselves into something resembling a more traditional unified chorus, which begins the progress towards the structured hymns (mirroring the newly structured society) sung at the play's end.

Second song (first stasimon): 321-96

The Furies have heard Orestes call to Athena for assistance and thus respond with their own form of special speech. The Binding Song, so called because with it the Furies intend to fix their victim in one place to prevent his further escape, warrants extended attention, not just because of its form and content, but because of (yet another) controversy over its staging and its unexpected connection to the later trial scene. The song, while designed to paralyze its object, centres more on a defence of their office and a denunciation of Apollo. They announce their theme while chanting in marching anapaests as they step into the formation they will use during their dance. But what is this formation and where, exactly, are they dancing? While there is some scholarly disagreement about whether choral dances were rectangular or circular, their first line (307), *age dê kai choron hapsômen*, seems best translated as 'come let us also join hands in a dance', which certainly suggests a circle which would enact the song's binding content.[23] Less certain is the position of Orestes and the ancient wooden effigy of Athena during the dance: they must either dance in a circle in the *orchêstra*'s middle and in front of Orestes who sits as a suppliant at Athena's statue, which is just in front of the *skênê*, perhaps on the *ekkyklêma*; or Orestes and the statue are in the *orchêstra*'s middle and the chorus dances around him. Based on the song's content and purpose, the latter seems more likely to me, but there are learned scholars who prefer the former.[24]

The primitive dark magic practised in this incantation may appear to be an intended stark contrast with the advanced, civilized mechanisms of the trial that follows it, yet recent scholarship has shown that Athenian trials in the classical era frequently featured magic. Faraone's important article deserves summary. The Binding Song 'is closely related to a specific kind of curse tablet used to affect the outcome of law cases in Athens as early as the fifth century BC', and thus it is importantly related to the dramatic context of *Eumenides*.[25] Curse tablets, which have been found wherever Greeks and Romans lived, were inscriptions on rolled or folded leaden sheets, most usually with the cursed person's name, which would be pierced with a nail in order to transfix the victim. Judicial curse tablets, one of the three main types that have been unearthed, were written prior to a trial's verdict, and aimed to hamper the antagonist's capacity to think and speak clearly during the trial. From early in *Eumenides* both the audience and the Furies know that there will be a court trial. Apollo tells first Orestes about the judges in Athens (81-2) and then the Furies about Athena's role in the trial (224). The Furies, as litigants, deploy the language of judicial curse: 'the song of the Furies which binds the mind' (331-2). Because trials in the civil courts often also involved political competition, curses could be particularly socially charged. This is true of Orestes' trial, for the Furies' ultimate target is not Orestes but Apollo, and hence the song's content focuses on the god, not his surrogate. If the Furies manage to bind both Orestes' mind and his tongue then he will lose and his divine protector will lose face.

Scene 3: 397-489

Athena enters from the left, finally, to interrupt the Furies' wild dancing. While there are certainly many prayers for divine assistance in Greek tragedy, Athena's actual response to Orestes' prayer is relatively unusual. Unlike most entrances, hers is unannounced, but Orestes, who had imagined her currently striding across Libya, near her birthplace, or on the Phlegrean plain, where the Olympians had battled the Giants (292-8), has summoned her. Even these small details foreshadow the coming events, since Athena's birth will feature in Apollo's arguments and the Giants were, like the Furies, primitive Chthonic beings who opposed the Olympians. Hesiod's *Theogony* (185) represents both Giants and Furies as born from Ouranos' blood and testicles after he was castrated by his son (and Zeus' father) Kronos. The reference to Libya here might have a topical significance in alluding to Athenian imperial activities, as will Athena's evocation of Troy, but such matters I reserve for my discussion of the politics of *Eumenides* in the next chapter.

Athena's arrival is thematically significant and a matter of staging in *Eumenides* that, once again, scholars contest. Every conceivable method and direction of entrance has received some support: on foot through the *skênê* doors, flying in from above on the *mêchanê* (a platform suspended by a crane), on foot from one of the sides, and from the side in a chariot.[26] Let us look at what the text has her say about her travels from Troy (403-5):

> From there I have come with a tireless step,
> whirring my aegis without wings,
> after I had yoked this chariot to strong horses

The dispute has arisen partly because these three lines seem to conflict with each other; line 405 indicates a horse-drawn chariot, while 404 indicates no such assistance, and 403 suggests a brisk march. Since the movement indicated in 403 could just be a figure of speech for any travel, those who see a conflict between 404 and 405 have proposed that one must have been added by an actor ('interpolated') during a later production. Yet most examinations of this passage neglect the strong structural parallels between this scene and Agamemnon's earlier arrival by chariot, accompanied by Cassandra, which are an important component of Athena's intervention. The long delay in Athena's appearance creates great tension, and it repeats, and reverses in a meaningful way, the similar lengthy delay in Agamemnon's appearance in the first part of the *Oresteia*.

The entry by chariot allows Aeschylus to have Athena to evoke simultaneously both Agamemnon and Cassandra.[27] Athena's words and stage actions reconnect her with Troy, and with the characters, events and metaphors of *Agamemnon*. She begins her speech in *Eumenides* by announcing that she has just returned from the 'land of Scamander', following the division of spoils among the Achaean leaders (397-402). Cassandra herself had been part of the previous distribution of Trojan plunder, and the *Oresteia* connects those two moments by having Athena describe the spoils as 'the choicest gift' (402), the exact same language, though slightly further embellished, that Agamemnon used of Cassandra when he arrived in Argos (*Agamemnon* 954-5). The symmetry of these words is underscored by their pronouncement by figures who have arrived into the acting area in chariots. Athena's arrival in the style and language of Agamemnon thus signals a reversal of the Argive king's destructive, hubristic homecoming, a large part of which involved Cassandra's final annihilation. Further, Athena's identification of Troy as the 'land of Scamander' might echo first the Herald's reference to it (*Agamemnon* 511) and then Cassandra's lament for her 'ancestral river of Scamander' (1157). In the *Libation Bearers*, Electra remembers the other warriors who died by the Scamander (366). The Scamander thus seems not just a geographical reference but also a source of pain inextricably bound up with the Trojan War. Athena now transforms the Scamander and Troy to a site of productive co-operation among Greek leaders. The harnessing of Troy's wealth for the god of the descendants of Theseus thus mirrors the larger use of the Trojan War myth in the *Oresteia* as part of the foundational myth of justice in Athens.[28] Athena arrives to solve the crisis of the House of Atreus that is now threatening to become an all-out war among the gods, so Aeschylus represents her as re-enacting, and thus repairing, the aftermath of Troy's fall that had led Orestes to commit matricide. But even if Athena merely strides into the acting area from the wings, her arrival from

Troy and her choice of words concerning her activities there will
still evoke that earlier entrance and its implications. As we
shall increasingly see, the second half of *Eumenides*, through
language, imagery and the iconography of its staging, reverses
Agamemnon's entrance.

Like Agamemnon, Athena finds herself immediately in a
scene of great tension, but unlike Agamemnon, she is able to
dissipate the force of the immediate conflict through her choice
of words and tone. Agamemnon had spoken of Troy's brutal
destruction and the need to quash any dissent of Argos before
even addressing, critically, his wife, while Athena's brief Trojan
tale mentions only its rewards, before she turns to notice her
suppliant and his pursuers. The Pythia's first sight of the
Furies has her recoiling in terror, and Apollo's first speech to
them bristles with violent hostilities, yet Athena is not afraid,
despite the astounding vision of this mob (407). Key to any
possibility of a settlement of this dispute is Athena's capacity to
serve as its impartial arbitrator (at least relatively speaking),
and she signals this immediately (408): 'Who are you? I speak
in common to all.' But clearly it is the Furies, not Orestes, who
attract her attention. As she begins to describe the Furies' form
she checks herself, almost as if she is aware of Apollo's earlier
taunts concerning their ugliness (413-14): 'When someone close
by speaks badly of another who is blameless, it is far from the
just and Right stands aside from it. '

'Right', the Greek *Themis*, is a particularly crucial term for
the *Oresteia*'s development, and harks back to its 'primal scene',
the sacrifice of Iphigenia. It is the final, and hence climactic,
word both in Athena's speech here and in the chorus' remembrance of Agamemnon's deliberation before killing his daughter
(*Agamemnon* 217). *Themis*, a word which occurs six times in the
Oresteia, denotes not what is right according to humans and
their morality, but according to divine law; thus Lloyd-Jones
translates Agamemnon's hope that the desire to sacrifice
Iphigenia is *themis*, 'right in the eyes of heaven'. Earlier, the
chorus, which is confused as to why Clytemnestra is suddenly
lighting so many sacrificial fires, asks her to tell them (97-8)

'whatever is both possible and *themis*'. Clytemnestra, almost
seeming to respond to Agamemnon's language while standing
over his corpse, cries to the shocked chorus of Argive elders
(1431): 'You also listen to this *themis* of my oaths'. This use of
themis, as commentators such as Fraenkel and Page lament, is
untranslatable; perhaps Smyth's old Loeb translation gets it
best with 'righteous sanction', since Clytemnestra immediately
moves in the next line to the *Dikê*, Justice, for her daughter's
death. At that moment, what is right and just is obviously in
dispute. As the gods themselves participate in *Oresteia*'s final
acts, its moral language begins to achieve greater certainty, and
now *themis* receives a clarity it lacked earlier. It cannot even be
themis to harm the blameless with words, let alone deeds. We
now know what is *themis* because a god herself tells us so. She
will also say that it cannot be *themis* for her to decide this
particular case by herself (471).

Under this rule of *themis*, Athena is able to engage the Furies
productively, and her respect for them enables the institution
of the trial. Athena proceeds quickly through a series of questions and requests for more information: Who are you? Tell me
your case clearly and I shall learn it. Is there any end to your
pursuit? Is this the one you hunt? Despite Orestes occupying
precisely the same endangered suppliant position that he did in
the first scene in Delphi, the contrast between her demeanour
and Apollo's is striking. Yet the seminal matter on which the
entire trial will turn is revealed when Athena responds to the
Furies' designation of the present suppliant as a matricide
whom they hunt (426): 'But was he under compulsion?' The
word for 'compulsion' here, *anankê*, also designates 'necessity',
and is also one of the key terms of the *Oresteia*'s first part. As
Athena's reference to *themis* recalls Agamemnon's delibera-
tions over the sacrifice of Iphigenia, *anankê* in turn evokes the
'yoke of necessity' (*Agamemnon* 218) that Agamemnon enters
after he accepts killing her. *Anankê* killed Agamemnon, but it
will, paradoxically, liberate Orestes. Orestes' relative freedom
of action becomes the central matter of Athena's consideration.

Athena continues that there are two sides to the suppliant's situation and his refusal to swear an oath of innocence has no bearing on the justice of the situation. In real Athenian trials, both defendant and prosecutor had to swear oaths of innocence and guilt respectively, and either side's refusal to do so auto- matically would forfeit a case. Orestes clearly cannot deny killing his mother, and admitting it would end the trial before it starts. Athena has not been told that Orestes was compelled by Apollo, yet she seems to suspect, perhaps because of the vehemence of the Furies' response, there is something extraor- dinary in this situation. She will hear further. What seems particularly interesting at this moment is the Furies' implicit desire both to be called just and to act justly (431): 'How so? Teach us; for you are not poor in wisdom.' The Furies thus agree to allow Athena to question Orestes and judge the case, fulfill- ing Apollo's promise (435): 'We reverence worthy deeds in return for worthy deeds.' Reverence and respect have been, and will continue to be, a driving motivation for the Furies,[29] who seem increasingly malleable to Athena's questioning until the trial commences and Apollo reappears with renewed bluster.

With the Furies' permission, Athena begins to interrogate Orestes, still mindful that the manner and content of her words must not antagonize them needlessly. Thus, she carefully avoids leading questions that point to the first substantive question she had asked the Furies, whether he had acted under compulsion, asking him instead for a more generic defence and identification of himself and his lineage. Yet an allusion to the myth of Ixion (441) might indicate her implicit interest in Orestes' intent, while still signalling her concern with his ritual status. A polluted suppliant would pose a danger at her altar and must be purified. She had previous experience with such a man, Ixion, who had killed either his father or his father-in-law (hence, the opposite of Orestes) and supplicated Zeus for cleans- ing. After Zeus consented, Ixion then attempted to rape Zeus' wife Hera, and Zeus punished him by eternally fixing Ixion to a burning wheel of fire. If this myth is implied in Athena's caution – and Apollo's repetition of Ixion as an example (717) suggests that Aeschylus wants his audience to think about this figure –

then here it would seem to suggest Athena's concern whether this suppliant will similarly repay the gods' generosity; the relationship between Orestes' character and his actions is thus again crucial.

Orestes' response tactfully ingratiates himself with his presumed judge. He quickly dispels her concerns with his possible pollution (443-52), repeating his earlier (276-86) account of his previous purifications. Orestes, though never naming himself (indeed he remains nameless until the Furies speak it at line 623), does identify himself first as Argive and then as the son of Agamemnon, 'with whom you made the Trojan city a city no longer' (455-8).[30] Clearly Orestes is proud of his father, but, at least to a modern audience, the first recollection of him as 'marshaller of the men of the fleet' (456) rings discordantly, since any reference to the collection of the armada against Troy inevitably brings Iphigenia to mind; not exactly Agamemnon's finest hour! The *Oresteia* has been at pains to erase his sister's memory in order to justify his mother's murder, but reminders manage to slip out at inconvenient moments. Even Apollo cannot simply whitewash Agamemnon, as he prefaces the account of his murder with the admission that he 'managed well for the most part' (631-2), before, again, designating him as a 'gatherer of ships'.

Orestes, however, is most concerned with renewing the alliance between his family and Athena, and seems to hope that their prior ties will help him in the trial. There may be in this exchange between Orestes and Athena the evocation of international aristocratic networks, thus closing ranks against the lower-class Furies.[31] Orestes then further flatters Athena with full credit for Troy's fall; in the Greek the pronoun *su*, 'you', is not needed and its presence is hence quite emphatic. Thus, having signalled his generational bond with Athena, he can next frame his murder of his mother in terms of harm done to his father, but also, by extension, to Athena herself.

Like his mother at the end of *Agamemnon*, Orestes does not deny the murder (463), but Clytemnestra, while admitting the deed, denies real responsibility for it (*Agamemnon* 1497-1508).

Orestes goes beyond even the Furies' earlier insistence that Apollo was completely (199-200, *panaitios*) and not partly (*metaitios*), responsible, but he further carefully closes his speech by picking up on Athena's question to the Furies about compulsion and the fear of someone's anger. Apollo does in fact now bear partial responsibility (465, *metaitios*) by threatening Orestes with physical punishment should he fail to act against those responsible (467, *epaitious*) for Agamemnon's death. I focus here on these iterations of compounds of the adjective *aitios*, which means 'responsible', for they show that the key issue in Orestes' trial is what caused him to murder his mother. Orestes does close his speech with a willingness to accept any verdict from Athena, and while it is tempting to then argue that he thus shows a greater acceptance of the trial mechanism than the Furies, who have not made quite such a complete concession (depending on how one reads line 434), he has played the ancestral-ties card and is at least hopeful that it is already part of a winning hand.

The stage is thus set, at least metaphorically, for the trial itself, which Athena now details in the latest surprise shift in direction, the third instance of a character in a 'double bind', and with words that have important implications for understanding how the vote will actually proceed. Apollo's instructions to Orestes (81-3) had not indicated that Orestes' judges would be humans, and not gods (which, as discussed earlier, was the tradition), an impression furthered by Apollo's taunts to the Furies (224) that Athena would rule over any trial; again, no mention of a human jury that might not be so amenable to potential Olympian deals behind the scenes. Let us look at the careful articulation of the goddess' concerns (470-9):

The matter is too great, if some mortal
thinks he can judge it; nor is it right (*themis*) even for me
decide the sides in a trial (*dikas*) for a murder full of such
    bitter anger,
especially since, you, for your part, broken like a horse,

as a purified, harmless, suppliant you have approached my
house,
but these females hold an allotted office not easily dismissed,
and, should they not meet with a victorious outcome,
then afterwards poison comes from their thoughts,
falling earthwards, unbearable, an endless sickness.

After Athena's next conclusion that both options are unmanage-
able for her, her initial announcement of the human jury is,
unfortunately, marred by an apparent substantial break in the
received manuscripts. Yet both situation and resolution are
unmistakable. For the third time in the trilogy, a character
enters into a 'double bind', a precarious place where both options in a crisis necessitate a bad event for their chooser. In
Agamemnon (206-17), Orestes' father had to choose between
killing his daughter in obedience to Artemis, thus also violating
the very ties of blood for which Orestes is being punished, and
disobeying Zeus, who wills the fall of Troy for the perfidy of
Paris. In *Libation Bearers* (269-96, 1030-2), Orestes was threatened both with his father's Furies by Apollo should he fail to
avenge Agamemnon, and with his mother's Furies should he
exact his revenge against her (924). While the maternal Furies
seem to be a detail Apollo left unmentioned in his threats,
Orestes himself, in freezing at the reality of killing his own
mother, entered into the same position as his father before him.
Athena now occupies this awkward place, yet unlike Artemis
and Apollo, she has less personally at stake in this matter.[32]
Moreover, she is both the deity in charge of deciding and the
figure in the double bind, and her lack of partisanship and dual
role help her see that, unlike the previous two situations where
the threat of punishment was the main motivating factor, right
exists on both sides; the wraths of the rejected suppliant and of
the Furies are real threats, but not the only factors. Even aside
from her concerns about the role of Orestes' choice in killing his
mother, Athena recognizes that he is a suppliant, with a sanc-
tified and protected status. The Furies also have their *moira*,

their position in the structure of the universe, which must be recognized.

Since neither any single mortal nor Athena alone can decide the matter, the only logical step is to hand it over to a *group* of mortals *organized* by Athena. She also perhaps gives slight acknowledgement that, as with Agamemnon's dilemma, her situation results from the workings of her father Zeus, for she prefaces her announcement of the jury by an acknowledgement, 'this matter has struck here like lightning', that is expressed with a verb, *epeskêpsen* (482) which elsewhere in Greek tragedy marks the lightning of Zeus hurled intentionally in response to human actions. [33] After the trial and the Furies' acceptance of their new role, Athena proclaims (973), 'Zeus Protector of Assemblies (*Agoraios*) has prevailed.' Athena thus perhaps implies here, ahead of Apollo's appearance, that she is not the only god with a direct line to the divine king. Judges will be chosen and oaths will be sworn. Athena departs, to the right, in her chariot,[34] with the promise (487-8): 'After I have selected the best of my citizens, I shall return, to decide this matter truly.'[35] It is important, I think, to recognize here that she is not delegating the decision to the jury entirely; she will be an active agent in deciding the outcome, not a passive presider. There will be a trial at a court that has not yet been indicated by Aeschylus as the Areopagus (unless it is so named in the lost lines from this speech). Orestes remains, or leaves. The Furies are free now to sing again.

Third song (second stasimon): 490-565

The third song divides *Eumenides* into two parts, as the artistic and moral orders of the second half emerge from the corresponding chaos of the first. The Furies begin to articulate their terse purpose ('we punish matricides') into a more coherent outlook on justice that resonates with the concerns of other characters and choruses in the *Oresteia*, and their song's poetic form also becomes more distinctly similar to other choral songs in the trilogy. They oscillate between maxims that should be comfortable and familiar to the audience, and more unsettling moments, such as laughter at their victims and a threat to walk away from enforcing justice should the trial's outcome be unacceptable to them.

Whereas previously the Furies' words had concentrated on the fact of their prosecution of Orestes, now they focus on the consequences of that prosecution's failure, and thus their principles. The audience has mainly been subject to the spectacle of the beleaguered suppliant hounded by this monstrous police force, and it is doubtless sympathetic to him. While the Furies were able to match Apollo in their first debate with him, they have had little chance to demonstrate why, despite the external compulsion Orestes felt, his matricide cannot be simply exonerated: if men can go unpunished for killing their mothers there is no crime they will not dare to commit. The acquittal of Orestes would nullify the Furies' office and they would cease to pursue wrongdoers. The Furies are not merely the agents of justice, they *are* Justice (511-16). This thought implies that any further evolution of justice will have to take them into account.

The Furies' words here reach back to earlier parts of the trilogy and forward to the imminent trial. Their proclamation of the benefits of Fear (*to deinon*, 517-25) anticipates parts of Athena's charter of the Areopagus (698): 'do not expel fear (*to deinon*) completely from the city'. The Furies ask what man or city would still 'show reverence for Justice' (*seboi Dikan*, 522-5) without the restraint of fear. Athena similarly announces that reverence (*sebas*) and fear will deter men from misdeeds (690-2). Even the Furies' next thought, that neither anarchy nor rule by despot is best, but rather the middle way, is matched by Athena (696-7). Moreover, a man should be just 'willingly, without compulsion' (*anankas*), and the role of compulsion was, of course, the first concern about the nature of Orestes' acts which Athena expressed. Since the correspondences between the principles of Athena and the Furies are multiple, Aeschylus must have intended the audience to notice them.

The metres and imagery of this song also reach back to the choral odes of *Agamemnon* and further suggest that the Furies are beginning to behave more like a normal chorus that expresses traditional wisdom. The metaphor of the submerged reef at 564 recalls *Agamemnon* 1005-6, while the abused altar of Justice at 539 harks back to *Agamemnon* 381-4. The extended metaphor of the shipwreck (553-65) further recalls the same image in *Agamemnon* (1005-14). The more traditional content of this song is appropriately expressed in metres that characterized the odes of *Agamemnon*.[36]

The first stanzas, with an articulation of order under their fearful presence, deploy a metre, lecythion, not heard since *Agamemnon*, which however fades by the third stanza as the Furies agitatedly sing more of fear and retribution. These shifts in form and content from the early songs enable Aeschylus to position the Furies as a moral force acceptable to his audience during the trial, which now begins.

Scene 4: 566-777

Even in this play, which presents so many staging issues, the trial of Orestes poses unprecedented challenges. We do not know whether this scene is set at the same locale as the previous one; whether Orestes has remained in the acting area; the size of the jury; when Apollo enters and exits; the exact totals of the vote and thus whether the jury's vote is a tie or a majority to convict; whether Athena's vote is actual or symbolic; how many people are in the acting area; and, last (I hope), who, exactly, is singing at the end. The nature of the vote is of paramount importance, but these other aspects will enter into our discussion as well.

First, we must establish the action's locale and what we see when this scene begins. Because of the presence of Athena's ancient statue, which was all that necessarily marked the area as Athens, the previous episode must have occurred on the Acropolis, near or at the site of what will become the Erechtheum, the temple of Athena Polias, which will later house the wooden image. As the trial begins, Athena tells all (685-90) that its site, the Areopagus, will continue to dispense

71

justice forever. Since the Areopagus lacked a temple of Athena, the scene must have changed. If Orestes did remain in the acting area during the last song (and nothing in the text marks him as leaving and entering), then such a scene change would be most remarkable, but, especially given the number of singular aspects of this play's dramaturgy, certainly not inconceivable; the chorus' song and the relatively blank acting area allow for a refocusing of the audience's perception on a new place.[37] The *skênê* continues to serve no function, and the audience's attention is drawn to the *orchêstra*, where stage hands will bring on a range of court paraphernalia, including a chair for Athena, the voting urns and benches on which the jury will sit, and where the jury and, possibly, additional silent extras will gather. The *orchêstra* is completely the focal point, where the debating, voting, counting, second debating and then final singing all will occur. As Hammond observes, the *orchêstra* 'is no longer just a large dancing place. It is the very city and land of Athens.'[38] If the large rock at the eastern edge of the *orchêstra* remained at the time of the *Oresteia*'s production, then it could have served to represent the Areopagus itself.[39] As the Furies end their song, Athena enters from the right (no doubt on foot this time), followed by a herald (see 566), trumpeter (567-9), and then, after the formal summons, ten or eleven jurors. It seems likely that Athena would sit at the *orchêstra*'s centre, with the jurors slightly behind her, the table and urn in front, and with Furies and Orestes each occupying one of the flanks, level with or slightly ahead of Athena.[40] Yet another unusual, if not unique, event is now occurring: a second group roughly the same size as the chorus has occupied the *orchêstra* and will remain there; as a result, at least spatially, 'the chorus has a rival'.[41] The characters Orestes, Apollo and Athena will address this rival in addition to or instead of the chorus of Furies, and indeed the three will, remarkably, interact with each other very little.

Typical theatrical practice comes further into question with Athena's addresses to her audience(s) and Apollo's final entrance. Let us consider the latter problem first. Apollo, since he is arriving from Delphi, would enter from the left, in contrast to Athena's right-hand entrance, from Athens. While there is always the possibility that the textual transmission from antiquity has left gaps in the received manuscripts, the surviving text, which seems reasonably sound here, shows that he both enters and leaves this scene unannounced, which would be unusual, but not impossibly so, yet also thematically appropriate. Athena suddenly addresses him (574-5): 'Lord Apollo, hold sway over what you own; tell me what's your part in this matter.' Athena politely, yet brusquely, manages her domineering half-brother. It would be impossible for the audience not to recognize a figure like Apollo as he enters, especially since he had appeared earlier, and hence an announcement of the identity of the new (in this scene) character would be unnecessary. Yet more ado about his appearance would also conflict with the pains Athena takes here to reduce his authority at this moment in her city.[42]

Another possibility offered by the theatre might also explain the odd way Aeschylus handles Apollo's arrival (and departure): he is not in the *orchêstra* but on the *skênê's* roof. Such is the suggestion in Meineck's translation, which was the product of attempts to recreate ancient production practice; while it is a distinctly minority opinion, this should not be dismissed casually.[43] While Apollo's presence there would distract from the new focus on the *orchêstra's* centre and thus disrupt the symbolism of the shift from the vengeful cycle of domestic violence represented by the *skênê*, such a disruption would in fact correspond to the effect his presence has on the civil proceedings. Once he engages the Furies in debate, the dialogue's tone is dragged back to the bitter harangues of the stalemate between them in Delphi. This staging is speculation, true, but not wild speculation.

Nonetheless, Apollo seems somewhat oblivious to, and perhaps surprised by, what he encounters, for, as he announces his intention to stand by Orestes as 'his advocate' because he shares the blame (*aitia*) for the murder, he instructs Athena to handle the matter herself: 'You, begin the proceedings as you know how, and determine the trial' (579-81). Apollo does here assume that Athena will be the sole judge, an assumption marked further by the single personal pronoun 'you' (*su*), which is grammatically unnecessary in the Greek. Apollo's presumption might also be a sign that he does actually enter precisely at 574, after having missed Athena's first address to the people during the previous four lines. Either way, Athena promptly ignores his advice, and begins the trial with the prosecution's brief.

Just before first addressing Apollo, Athena instructs her herald to 'call the public to order', yet this simple command raises further questions of who exactly is in the acting area and whether Aeschylus is involving his audience in the performance of the trial scene. Which people need to be called to order? One might suggest a large crowd of extras, but that seems unlikely.[44] The smallish jury seems unlikely to be called 'the public' and certainly would not need to be instructed thus. The only remaining possibility is that the public are the audience sitting in the theatre that day. Athena does not 'know' she is addressing real, living Athenians, but Aeschylus is inviting them into the world of the play so that they can understand the institution of the Areopagus by participating in it. As Sommerstein puts it, 'from the point of view of the play, they are the Athenians *of the future* whom Athena thrice says she is addressing (572, 683, 707-8)'.[45] Thus at this moment, and later, Athena speaks directly to all of Athens, not just to the jury.

Both in presenting their case and in attacking Orestes' defence, the Furies prove themselves remarkably effective trial lawyers. Instead of a prosecution speech, which would have slowed down the play considerably, they move to directly confronting their antagonist, with a promise to 'speak succinctly' (585). In eighteen lines of rapid-fire *stichomythia* (single-line dialogue) the Furies, presumably through the chorus leader, move Orestes through an immediate confession (588), to assigning responsibility to their real target Apollo (594), and then finally forcing Orestes into the problematic position that he is not related to his mother by blood (606). This is prompted when, in trading accusations about his family's murderous history, Orestes returns the debate to the limited scope of the Furies' pursuit of only those who shed kindred blood (605-6): 'Am I from my mother in blood?' The Furies' incredulous response, in a couplet that climaxes and breaks the *stichomythia*, was probably shared by the audience, and Orestes, backed into a seemingly indefensible corner, begs Apollo to take over the debate (609-13). Orestes himself falls silent until the votes are counted.

Apollo does not seem to fare much better, relying on a seemingly random sequence of forensic attacks, each of which his opponent parries successfully. First, he claims the authority of Zeus in all his words is so great that it exceeds any oath (614-21), including, presumably, the one the jurors swore at Athena's bidding. If the jury votes against Orestes, and, by extension, Apollo, they oppose, by further extension, Zeus himself. The rule of the father, both Agamemnon and Zeus, increasingly becomes central to Apollo's argument, as Apollo stresses the greater sanctity of the male hero of the Trojan war, cut down by his treacherous wife, who thus had to be killed herself, but with justice. Apollo thus seems to walk right into a snare that the Furies have not even bothered to lay out properly (640-1): 'A father's death, according to your argument, Zeus honours first, but he himself bound his elder father, Kronos.' Hesiod's *Theogony* (716-35) had depicted the decade-long war between the Olympians and the generation of their parents, the Titans, who were finally confined deep in Tartarus. Greeks would have known this story from infancy. That the example of Zeus' treatment of Kronos was probably a stock argument in debates about patriarchal justifications in human morality is shown by its appearance, a few decades later, in both Aristophanes' *Clouds* (902-6) and Plato's *Euthyphro* (6a). Apollo, then, defeated, resorts to several lines of insult, as he had back in Delphi, followed by another mythological oversight (647-51), that father Zeus did not invent any magic incantations to provide for resurrection for a man once he is dead. Actually, in a myth already alluded to in *Agamemnon* (1022-4), Zeus destroyed Apollo's mortal son Asclepius for resurrecting a human being.[46] This is not the only instance in the debate where Apollo plays loose with well-known stories, and indeed, in the Delphi scene he had specifically argued that the examples of gods could be used to discuss the propriety of human actions (213-18). Moreover, he has just handed another argument to the Furies, for his insistence on the finality of human bloodshed allows the prosecutors to re-emphasize Orestes' permanent pollution for matricide.

Apollo is now cornered, as Orestes was, and, as Orestes did, he lunges after the most extreme argument he can make, denying any blood relationship between a mother and the children who emerge from her body (657-61). This passage is one of the most notoriously controversial in all of Greek literature. I shall deal with the currency of and background to Apollo's claims about maternity in Chapter 6, but for now I shall point out some important aspects of this argument's dramatic context. First (and again), Apollo's debating strategy, if he has one, has not been working, and he is now desperate. Second, at least half of the jury does not accept this argument and so votes to convict Orestes of shedding his mother's blood. Third, this argument does not rebut the Furies' claim that the mother nourishes an embryo with her blood, and even concedes her function as a nurse (659).[47] Fourth, even his claim that Athena, his sole piece of evidence, was 'not nurtured in the shadows of a womb' (665), ignores her initial conception by the goddess Mêtis, an early lover of Zeus, before Zeus swallowed her in fear of a prophecy that she would bear a son greater than his father (*Theogony* 886-900). One can only imagine how Aeschylus staged the Furies' physical reaction to the denial of maternity, for, after Apollo concludes with a bribe to the jury of an alliance between Orestes' descendants and Athens (668-73), Athena quickly steps into the fray and stops the discussion.

Why Athena intervenes here must be considered. The irony of the extremity of Apollo's final argument is that it does provide Athena with an appropriate entry point to ask, quite tactfully, whether discussion has been sufficient to allow for a

vote. Apollo admits he has nothing left with an archery metaphor, that all of his arrows have been shot (676). Now she turns
to the Furies (678): 'What can I do to be blameless in your eyes?'
It is unclear from the Furies' reply whether they ignore Athena
or (as I would suggest) include her in the jury (679-80): 'You
(plural) heard what you (plural) heard, but, while casting your
votes keep reverence in your heart, strangers.' The word *xeinoi*,
'strangers', here could be a biting glance at Apollo's assertion
that the mother keeps the embryo 'like a stranger to a stranger'
(*xenôi xenê*, 660).[48] The pithy, yet snarling, 'you heard what you
heard', also seems somehow directed primarily at Apollo's extreme claim. 'What more could we say?' they seem to suggest.
Why Athena then accepts Apollo's side I shall postpone until the
appropriate place.

Athena, however, does not proceed immediately to the vote,
but to the eternal ordinance of the Areopagite tribunal for
Athens. I shall examine the exact nature and function of this
speech in relation to the real Areopagus in the next chapter, but
for now let us look briefly at how Athena's concerns and language resonate in the drama's large themes. 'Areopagus'
literally means 'the hill of Ares', where the Athenian hero
Theseus defeated Amazons who had invaded Athens in search
of their queen Antiope (or Hippolyta), whom Theseus had taken
as a prize following their defeat. The Amazons, a tribe of
barbarian female warriors, used the Areopagus as a base to
attack the Acropolis, as did the Persians earlier in Aeschylus'
life (Herodotus 8.25.1). As Lysias (2.4) and Isocrates later write,
their father was Ares, so sacrifice to him there before battle
(*Eumenides* 689) would have been appropriate. Theseus' conquest of the Amazons would thus foreshadow Orestes' of the
Furies, yet Athena quickly steers the court's charter away from
the discourse of victory and defeat, since, as discussed earlier,
Athena's vision of justice in Athens under the Areopagus con-
sists of concepts and language that the Furies had articulated
in their song before the trial (690-706): respect, reverence, fear,
the middle. Athena gives the instructions for her court not to its
first members, but to 'the Attic people' (681) and 'the citizens for

the future' (708). The jury must 'arise, take a voting pebble and decide the trial, while respecting your oath' (709-10). Since Apollo had earlier urged the jury that Zeus' word has precedence over any oath, Athena in closing the proceeding reminds the jury that this is her court, not his. The vote now begins, and how it unfurls is an immensely complex matter, so let us step back and consider it in detail and in terms of the larger picture.

At this point in my discussion of *Eumenides* it should be clear that, in every scene, there are fundamental uncertainties concerning its staging, and that these uncertainties have no small effect on how we can understand the meaning of its action. The trial of Orestes is the scene most fraught with these ambiguities. Our dilemma revolves around the number of people present and voting in the trial. Controversy surrounds the questions of whether the number is odd or even, and whether Athena's vote is actual or symbolic. If the number is even, then Athena's vote in favour of Orestes is superfluous, and the tied vote of humans itself acquits, but, if the number is odd, then Athena's vote is real and meaningful, producing the tie; in other words, the human jury is not convinced and compulsion has no role in determining guilt and innocence. It should be quickly apparent how essential this small detail is. Eminent scholars have reached contrary conclusions based upon the available evidence, and I shall attempt to present both cases evenly before establishing my own proposal. Scholarly consensus has the ten couplets spoken by Apollo and the Furies (711-30) representing ten jurors coming forward to vote, but there is sharp disagreement about whether the succeeding triplet (731-3) marks the final eleventh vote or the time Athena needs to move forward for her announcement.[49] I shall not rehearse in great detail the arguments concerning the jury size, not least because they are well summarized in Sommerstein's commentary, save to point out that arguments for an even number of jurors tend to rely too much on external evidence.[50] My concern will be with a close reading of the text and its implied stage action.

It is only by paying close attention, imaginatively, to the implied performance of Orestes' trial in *Eumenides* that we can decide, definitely I hope, the number of jurors, understand the nature of their vote and Athena's intervention, and precisely why the Furies become so enraged. The acquittal of Orestes is *the* crux of the *Eumenides* and indeed perhaps of the *Oresteia* as a whole and the question of *how* Orestes is acquitted is inseparable from the question of *why*.

So what do we know about the quantity of jurors and how do we know it? Any conclusion must be drawn inferentially, because Aeschylus at no point signals unambiguously the number of votes that are cast, and the jurors themselves are silent. We know that the votes will be placed in two urns (742), which must be large enough to be visible at a distance in the theatre and marked so that characters and audience can distinguish guilty from innocent. A clear stage action is imperative. Athena orders that the vote commence (708-10), followed by much arguing and commenting by the combatants (who are not voting), followed by Athena's command to spill the urns' contents and count the vote (742-3). Between lines 710 and 742 the jurors place their votes in the urns, but no character says as much during those 32 lines. An unorganized stroll by each juror during those 32 lines seems unlikely in an artistic medium where order and symmetry are such paramount concerns, so attention must focus on the role of the sequence of ten couplets (711-33) spoken by the Furies (or their leader) and Apollo, with a final triplet by the chorus. Each couplet would mark the time it takes for a juror to step forward and place his vote in one of the two urns. Since Athena announces that the final vote is a tie and the combatants speak in turns, no other scenario seems likely than having each vote placed in an alternating urn as the speakers trade turns. This sequence suggests a jury of ten. The final triplet would either mark the climatic and deciding vote by an eleventh juror or the time it takes for Athena to step forward to the urns with her own decision. The decision which of the two is more likely rests on clues in the rest of the scene, most of which involve Athena's role.

The content of these couplets further demonstrates the urgency of the trial's resolution. Furies and Apollo return to aggressively taunting one another over the murder and their relative domains, and they thus threaten to drag the play back to the trilogy's earlier parts. Neither side seems to have learned anything from the trial's first part. The first couplets by each side even threaten the jury with harm should they not decide in the speaker's favour, and Apollo continues to hide behind Zeus. Apollo persists in distorting mythology by evoking the paradigm of Zeus' purification of the suppliant Ixion, the first murderer, claiming that his father's decision to do this means it must be correct, while glossing over the fact that Ixion subsequently abused the mercy of Zeus by trying to rape Hera (and was not one of Apollo's earlier arguments about the importance of the sacred bonds of marriage between Zeus and Hera?). The Furies' terse response could signal they recognize the folly of this example: 'You say so' (719). The Furies also allude to Apollo's victory over another group of females, the Fates, when he made them drunk in his attempt to save Admetus from an early death.

The rage of the self-centred justifications on each side prompts Athena's intervention with particularly pointed words before she announces her support for Orestes. Athena prefaces this statement thus (and my awkward word order attempts to preserve the force of the Greek, 734): 'Mine is this here function, to be the last one to decide the trial.' 'Mine' (*emon*) signals her reiteration that this court is *hers*. 'And *I* (a very emphatic, because grammatically unnecessary, pronoun *egô*) add this here voting pebble for Orestes' (735). 'This here' (*tênde*) indicates she holds up a pebble for all to see, but whether at this moment she physically places the pebble in the urn for innocence is unclear. Either she immediately drops it into the urn and produces the tie or she holds it in reserve in case he is convicted by one vote. We cannot tell by this single line, but the edge to her language, her insistence on *her* job as the *final* one, suggests to me that her vote is very real. But others disagree. On the other hand, her decision is clear (736-41):

For there is no mother who gave birth to me,
and I approve the masculine in all things, save for
    accepting marriage,
with all my heart, and I am very much my father's.
Therefore, I shall not honour preferentially the death of a
    woman
who killed her husband who was the caretaker of the
    household.
Orestes is victorious, even if his case is decided with equal
    votes.

Such reasoning has dismayed, and continues to do so today, more than just the Furies, and yet Aeschylus presents a goddess who carefully weighs what evidence is available and then with equal care explains her reasoning. One must remember here that Athena is in a double bind that will require all her divine powers to manage successfully. First, however, it is important to note what she does *not* say here. Athena omits any reference to the role of compulsion, which seemed to be her earlier concern, though her weighing of the deaths of father and mother perhaps nods in that direction. She also does not deny the blood relationship between mother and child, which was the primary component of Apollo's introduction of her as evidence in support of Orestes, nor draw any kind of universal conclusion from it.[51] She is being asked to decide whether the response to the murder of a father by murdering in turn the mother can in anyway be justified, and she chooses to accept it based upon the father's greater importance as 'the caretaker of the household'. Her birth from her father means she cannot give preference to the death of a mother who is second to the father in significance for the household. The catastrophe of Agamemnon's death for the house and the salvation of that house through Clytemnestra's death have both been consistently articulated throughout the *Oresteia*, and are re-emphasized in Orestes' first words after the verdict is announced. Apollo's decision to use Athena as an example of the priority of paternity gives Athena an entry point to save Orestes, but in a way that allows her to avoid offending

81

the Furies more than is absolutely necessary. She does not deny the Furies' arguments, nor does she really agree with Apollo's, but rather forges her own middle way. She takes the mantle of Zeus' spokesman away from Apollo in these lines, while also asserting her independence, for her exception to the rule of the father, 'save for accepting marriage', is not a small one, and indeed her exception undercuts the justification of her paternal birth and shifts the burden to the father's role as protector of the household. Like the Furies, Athena does not marry, but the former seem to belong totally to the mother. Again, Athena finds a middle way and votes for Orestes.

But it remains unclear what, exactly, her vote actually does and whether the vote is notional or real. Let us backtrack a bit and look at the essential information again. My central operative assumptions here are that all aspects of the voting are visible to the characters, especially the divine ones, and to the audience, and the text should signal them clearly. But any discussion of the vote is problematized by the seemingly scanty information the text yields about it. Central aspects, such as the size of the jury, must be drawn from the couplets from 711-30 (or 711-33, if one includes the triplet). From 708-10 Athena does clearly indicate that the vote commences, and it does seem sensible, if not unavoidable, to conclude that, at each insult and threat traded by Furies and Apollo, a single juror comes forward to vote; indeed the controlled order of the couplets and movements of the jurors, in contrast to the violent language of the opposing deities, enacts the larger movement of the trilogy from vendetta to legal system and the rule of law.

Yet scholars have not really considered the implications of the function of the two urns here (742). I know this sounds painfully obvious: the urns are there to receive the votes. But my focus is on the number two. What is required is a visible and meaningful stage action. Aeschylus could have staged the vote with a single urn and given each juryman two voting instruments, one for guilty, one for innocent, so that the ballots would be secret. That he did not indicates that he wants the nature of each vote to be visible to all, and therefore each couplet surely

4. The Play and its Staging

marks a voting pebble (709, 735) placed in the urn designated for the side of the couplet's speaker.[52] The vote's clarity would thus evoke an Attic vase of 480 BC that represents the balloting concerning the awarding of the arms of Achilles to Ajax or Odysseus, a vote that was also overseen by Athena, where 'jurors' are depositing their pebbles in two very obvious piles.[53] The audiences on the stage and in the theatre thus know that at 730, when the last couplet is spoken by Apollo, the jury is deadlocked, thus increasing the tension enormously over what seems, to me at least (but, I stress, not to everyone), the likely scenario, that the chorus' triplet (731-3) marks the final and convicting vote. The decisiveness, however temporary it ultimately is, of this last vote seems the best explanation for the shift to the triplet here. Otherwise, why not simply move to Athena immediately upon the completion of Apollo's last couplet? Why give the Furies the first and the final words and thus yield eleven and not ten statements, a number that grows to a dozen if Athena is included?

The number twelve indeed might be quite significant here, as the couplets in the vote recall and reverse the shattering of community represented by the dozen couplets after Agamemnon's murder (*Agamemnon*, 1346-71). The vote mirrors the debate among Argive elders about what action to pursue against Agamemnon's murderers.[54] It is both possibly significant and possibly coincidental that the twelve individual voices of the chorus in *Agamemnon* match the number of votes in Orestes' trial, but the orderly array of the latter transforms the chaotic dozen unleashed by Agamemnon's murder. In *Eumenides*, the constructive division of lines builds the city of Athens in the form of its new means of assuring the rule of law, even as the chorus' fracturing in *Agamemnon* enacted the dissolution of the body politic of Argos. Moreover, the legal language that immediately explodes anew in *Agamemnon* through the chorus' denunciations of Clytemnestra foreshadows and is transformed by the third play's truly juridical scenario; one Argive elder even speaks of 'casting a voting-pebble to do something' (*Agamemnon* 1353).

The violently hostile confrontation between chorus and female protagonist following the vote then recalls and transforms the one following Agamemnon's death as the female is able to persuade, not threaten with force, the angry chorus that confronts her, who in the first play would put her on trial if it could. The third chorus then does not slink off in silence, its voice suppressed, but finds a new joyful voice, not displaced by a silent gang of armed thugs but joined by a new chorus of singers. The transformative structural echoes all suggest, I submit, that the twelve-step exchange between Furies, Apollo and then Athena answers the collapse of the chorus of Argive elders into twelve individual voices at the murder of King Agamemnon. Unlike the parallel moment in *Agamemnon*, effective agents and contesting speakers are separated, further embodying the removal of authority from the individual to the community. Moreover, if the dozen voiced opinions in the trial echo the twelve after the murder, then Athena's vote would surely be integral, not ornamental, since hers would be the twelfth.

That Athena has been watching this vote unfold explains why she intervenes in the manner she does. The central word of the chorus' triplet – the first word of its second line – is the centrally thematic *dikê*, which Athena echoes at the end of her next line. 'We wait to hear the verdict (*dikês*).' 'My task here is to decide the final verdict (*dikên*).' Yet this statement echoes and contradicts Athena's earlier demurral (471-2), 'it is not right (*themis*) to decide verdicts (*dikas*) of murder that bring quick anger'. Her vote does precisely that, immediately incurring the rage of the Furies. And she knows what she is doing, as shown by the emphatic 'Mine is the task' that initiates the explanation of her vote, a decision she had said she would not make. Yet now she has watched both the arguments and the vote and she knows she must act, even if it might be interpreted as violating *themis*, not exactly a neutral word in the *Oresteia*; however, her invocation of *themis* earlier involved her deciding the case by herself.

If the votes were in fact patently equal then she would not

need to proclaim hers *and* then add (741) that an equal vote means acquittal. Only if the votes are visibly odd in number will Athena's be meaningful, and this might explain Apollo's final line (perhaps) that 'a single vote restored a house'.[55] All translations of this line have Apollo say 'a single vote can restore a house', and my point here, shifting the translation from present to past, is too technical for this discussion.[56] I still must acknowledge that Athena's lines 734-41 can support both the interpretation that she votes as the twelfth jury member and that she presents a 'casting' vote that merely ratifies the even draw as it is announced, but the text itself seems to indicate more the former position. In line 735, Athena appears to announce her vote for Orestes unconditionally, while a 'casting vote' would need to be articulated conditionally; i.e. she does not say 'I will vote for Orestes *if* the other votes are equally divided.' Moreover, at 753, when the result is announced, she does not even hint that her own vote is not included, and she announces the acquittal first and the equal vote second, 'an unnatural order if at the same time she is seen adding her own vote to one of the piles so as to destroy the equality of votes and bring about the acquittal'.[57] Athena thus fulfils the promise of her earlier decision to accept the institution of the trial, that this matter is too important for mortals to judge alone, nor right for her alone. She has been conducting this trial *with* the human jury, and she several times insisted on her direction of *her* court.

Orestes' reaction to the verdict could also indicate whether Athena's vote has actively produced the tie (754-6):

O Pallas, you have saved my house
and you have put me back in the land of my fathers
when I had been deprived of them.

Orestes is quite emphatic that it is Pallas Athena, not the human jury, who has saved him. Indeed, he does not mention the jury at all, and his words strongly emphasize the agency of the goddess. Athena's last word before his outburst, *palôn* (votes), echoes in Orestes' cry of 'Pallas', almost producing a punning new epithet, 'Pallas of the Votes'.[58] His statement that she has restored him to his ancestral lands uses the quite emphatic (again because grammatically unnecessary) pronoun *su*. It might be surprising that Orestes then pledges an alliance to Athena's city after its jury has voted against him, but his own words stress repeatedly that his fealty is to the physical land and the city of Pallas ('to this land and your city', 762; 'city of Pallas', 772) and not just the city itself. His hero's tomb (766-71) will protect Athena's city even after his death.[59]

A common complaint against Athena's vote after the humans have elected to convict is 'we would expect Orestes to be indignant with the Athenians and extremely grateful to Athena', if Athena's vote had resulted in the tie.[60] Yet it would seem at least as likely that a man in Orestes' situation would be so relieved as to overlook the humans who voted against him, and Aeschylus' focus here needs to move quickly to the more pressing matter of the Furies' reaction. All that would matter for Aeschylus' purpose is the result. Orestes' speech itself, indeed, looks to the future and moves from the past as quickly as possible. His praise is for Athena, and not for the inhabitants of her city.

This focus by Orestes on Athena, not Athens, becomes especially clear once we consider the speed of his exit and the mystery concerning Apollo's departure. Orestes concludes his speech at 777 and marches off quickly to the left, towards Argos. But the audience has not heard from Apollo since line 751 (most likely), and the text gives no indication of his reaction to the favourable verdict. Moreover, he makes no farewell statement, and nobody notices him leaving. This is all quite odd in any context, but especially according to Greek theatrical conventions.[61] As the text stands, Apollo enters and leaves silently, unannounced, and this very symmetry is one argument for accepting the exit. As indicated earlier, Meineck's translation, based on theatrical experience, proposes Apollo's presence on the *skênê* roof, which would allow for a quick arrival and departure. Scholars have proposed five solutions for this uncertainty.[62] (1) Apollo exits between 753 and 754, after

Athena ends her proclamation and before Orestes speaks. Because the audience's focus shifts to Orestes, Apollo can slip away unnoticed. This would be unconventional, not to mention uncharacteristic of the Aeschylean Apollo. (2) Apollo exits with Orestes after 777, but this answer does not resolve the question of his silence. (3) Apollo leaves sometime during Orestes' speech, a suggestion that solves little. (4) Apollo stays in the acting area until the play's end, a theory that makes little sense dramatically and thematically. (5) There is an unnoticed gap in the manuscripts we have received, and the play's missing part contained Apollo's exit; no evidence supports this theory. Glenn Most then proposes re-assigning lines 775-7 to Apollo on the grounds that they make more sense coming from the god and provide him with an appropriate departure alongside Orestes; ancient manuscripts contained the barest indications of changes in speakers. This argument makes much sense, especially since it would have the last word from Apollo be 'victory-bearing' (*nikêphoron*), one that would credibly set off the Furies' immediate rants against 'the young gods' in the next line. But this new arrangement would not answer the concern that Orestes' speech neglects Apollo's role in his salvation, which thus implies Apollo has already left.[63] Moreover, assigning these lines to Apollo would result in a shorter speech by Orestes that thanks Athena and her city, not its people; the only direct reference to the Athenian people after the trial comes from the mouth of Apollo at 775, as Apollo says goodbye to 'you and the city's people'. Nonetheless, Apollo and Orestes are now gone. Athena is left alone with the Furies (and, we should not forget, a crowd of extras).

Fourth song and scene 5: 778-end

The quick assumption that *Eumenides* is only about the trial of Orestes is easily shown wrong when one simply considers that, after Orestes leaves the acting area, roughly one quarter of the play remains. The final scene of *Eumenides* is in fact longer than the trial scene itself. Form here will follow function. This drama's structure suggests that, more than deciding Orestes' fate, more than the institution of the Areopagus, the purpose of the drama's action is to depict the installation of these goddesses in the Athenian Acropolis. Helen Bacon states this matter eloquently: 'The *Oresteia* culminates not, as one might expect, in the resolution of the problems of Agamemnon's heir in Argos, but in the establishment of a chorus of Furies in a new home in Athens ... In this final scene, the emphasis shifts ... from the problems of Argos and the house of Atreus to the Furies' role in the cosmos and Athens' role in clarifying it.'[64]

In depicting this transformation, Aeschylus' dramatic imagination remains bold and innovative until the final lines, continuing to integrate the drama's content with its form. The Greek tragic poet's normal structural technique divides scenes of action by choral songs. After line 777 Aeschylus presents a sequence of two larger lyric passages (778-891 and 916-1020) that centre around the 24 lines consisting of two speeches by Athena and dialogue between her and the Furies where she finally persuades their acceptance. In those two lyric passages, with their agitated emotional metres of the earlier odes, the repeated stanzas sung by the chorus are answered by Athena, who speaks in the iambic metre.[65] Aeschylus had used such a technique in *Agamemnon* to mark the discord first between Cassandra and the Argive elders and then between them and Clytemnestra, but Aeschylus deploys this form here to a different end, as Athena's calm speech aims not to confuse or oppose the chorus, but to win it over. The repetitions of stanzas in the Furies' songs depict the determination in their emotional response to the verdict in seeming obliviousness to the arguments made during the trial, and the very repetitiveness shows their complete unwillingness to consider any justification for the votes against them. Their shift from singing into speech at 892 signals they are ready to listen and to change. The clash between song and speech in this scene would have evoked the ending of *Agamemnon*, where the chorus is defeated, brutally repressed by Clytemnestra and Aegisthus, and slinks off in silence. In *Eumenides*, however, the song begins anew and

differently, and chorus joins the singing actor in new, harmoni-
ous lyrics. There is virtually no action for the drama's last
quarter, just speech and song.

Another Aeschylean twist on expectations is his reversal of
the normal structure of the suppliant drama. In such a play, a
fugitive asks for sanctuary against a persecutor from a host in
a new city, and, after suppliancy is granted, the persecutor is
repulsed and leaves, while the protected suppliant remains.[66]
The Furies, during the trial (711,720), had made it quite clear
that an unfavourable outcome would provoke them to blight the
Athenian land, so every expectation would be for Athena to try
to persuade them to leave as quickly as possible. Instead, not
only does the suppliant Orestes depart to return to his old
home, but his persecutors the Furies remain, and, at his protector's bidding, move into their new home. Among the *Oresteia*'s
many surprises, this might be the greatest and most important
coup pulled off by Aeschylus; while Apollo tells Orestes and the
Furies that they will travel to Athens to be judged by Athena,
Aeschylus does not give the slightest hint that the terrifying
monsters at Delphi will become the beneficent deities at Athens, who will end the trilogy singing the praises of Athena, Zeus
and Athens. So let us now look in detail at how the resolution
of the *Oresteia*'s final crisis unfolds.

The chorus of Furies, after a stunned silence while Orestes
does his verbal victory lap around the *orchêstra*, erupts in shock
and rage. Following Athena's proclamation of acquittal (752),
the Furies, whether simply because of the scale of Orestes'
jubilant speech or because they are unable to respond, do not
commence their song for 25 lines (778), and this song launches
with an attack on 'the young gods (*neôteroi theoi*) who ride their
horses roughshod over the old laws', which signals, I think, the
real source of their unhappiness: Athena's intervention, in
support of Apollo.[67] Indeed she later calls herself by the Furies'
adjective for her: *neôteras*, younger. Their choice of an eques-
trian metaphor here would point back to the horse-drawn
chariot on which Athena most likely first entered. They do use
the same image at two earlier places (150, 731), one before and

one after Athena's entrance, but Athena is the god most associated with horsemanship and her entrance fixes the association firmly in the minds of both chorus and audience. While there could be in these lines a tension between the 'lower-class' Furies and the 'upper-class' Olympians, since horse-riding had particularly strong aristocratic associations,[99] whether these associations directed the audience's sympathy is unclear.

What is clear is that the Furies now threaten to unleash blight and plague on the Athenian land (782-7), and the stakes for Athens are visibly enormous, since, as it is so easy to forget while reading, the acting area is filled with Athenian citizens. These are not abstract threats, but ones directed at people in full view of the audience: the jury members, the best of Athena's citizens, the rival silent chorus that had competed for the actors' attention during the trial. Those unspeaking jury members have now taken Orestes' place, and, in order to defend them, Athena likely has moved forward in the *orchêstra* to meet the Furies during their first song and dance. Hammond imagines the scene vividly: 'They circle round Athena standing at the altar as they had circled around Orestes, and the Judges, the Crowd and the citizens in the theatre shrink back in terror, for the survival of their country is at stake.'[69] They do not threaten Athena directly because they know they cannot, and any assault would be ineffective. Indeed, they never directly attack Apollo, their true antagonist, preferring to work through his protégé. A model for the Furies' anger can be found in the Homeric *Hymn to Demeter*, as that goddess directs her final rage not against Zeus, whom she cannot affect directly, but against the fertility of the earth, which supports the humans who worship him and the other Olympians (305-13). Like Demeter, the Furies are only fully appeased by the promise of new honours.[70]

The Furies had agreed to the trial out of respect for Athena's wisdom and reverence (430-5), and their pre-trial song articulated a vision of justice that remarkably resembles what Athena formulates after the trial. Mutual respect and shared ideas lead their anger to subside for a while. Save not for Apollo's goading, they might remain remarkably calm through the trial. Now, instead, 'I am dishonoured' (780), and their sense of respect from Athena is gone. Their rage becomes renewed and redirected at Athena (with Apollo certainly gone before, 777) because, while there never seems to be any doubt in their minds that they might lose, they do then watch the vote proceed, with five or six votes cast in their favour, and believe they have won. Indeed, since Athena does not articulate the principle that a draw yields a victory for the defendant until after the vote, the Furies might assume that equal votes would lead to the prosecution winning. Athena watches the jury and reacts with her intervention, and the Furies watch first the jury, then Athena, and react to her reaction, which seems to run contrary to her earlier promise. Athena signals her awareness of her move's untenability by dropping its debatable justifications – that mothers lack a blood tie to their sons and that she thus sides with the male in all matters – and shifting the focus very quickly to the process and its conclusion (795-6): 'You are not defeated, but the result of the verdict of equal votes truly is not to your dishonour.'

By denying the language of victory and defeat that had characterized the struggles of the entire *Oresteia*, Athena hopes to remove the concept of dishonour before announcing the Furies' new honours. She transfers the responsibility Apollo had claimed to Zeus himself (797-9), careful not to mention Apollo by name, before promising them a new home and honours. Unmoved, they repeat their lament (808-22), and Athena realizes she must counter the core of the rage, their sense of dishonour (810) in her second reply's first line: 'You are not dishonoured' (824). Following a brief nod at her access to Zeus' thunderbolt – a weapon she will not use, unlike the violence wielded against Troy – Athena now begins to detail the rewards of accepting her offer, rewards that further heal the societal ruptures of *Agamemnon*. Instead of sacrifices *of* children, there will be one *before* their birth. Instead of a war that will serve as the perverted bloody rite before marriage (*proteleia*: *Agamemnon* 65, 227, 720), there will be true marriages. Some slight progress might be indicated by the Furies' decision to sing a new stanza, not a second repetition of the first, which, while it acknowledges Athena's offer, still obsesses on their dishonour (839, 845). Athena notices the mixture of acknowledgement and obstinacy, and so she expands her conception to link Athens' honour to the Furies'. Because Athens will become more honoured (853) as time passes, her people will be able to grant the Furies ever-greater honours (855-7), but this cannot happen if the Furies blight her land. They reply by repeating the third stanza.

Athena's final stratagem involves further transformation of language and themes from the entire trilogy. The Furies had suffered their first defeat earlier in the play because Orestes had greater stamina than they, who first appeared asleep in Apollo's temple, and Athena signals now her even greater capacity for endurance (891): 'I shall not grow tired of telling you the benefits'. Athena uses the Furies' obsession with 'reverence' (*sebas*, 885) in service of Persuasion, *Peithô*, which throughout the *Oresteia* has been a deeply problematic, if not sinister, force, as seen especially in Clytemnestra's persuasion of Agamemnon to walk on the tapestries, Pylades' persuasion of Orestes to kill his mother, and Apollo's arguments during the trial.[71] Now, with the link between *eros* and persuasion from Clytemnestra uncoupled in the virgin Athena, persuasion is used without deceit or threat of violence and solely for the common good, not for any private agenda. For an audience in a society where the ability to persuade in the law courts and the Assembly was paramount to individual success, this transformation surely is central to Aeschylus' final hope for a better Athens. By appealing to reverence and honour, Athena now can turn the table, so that the choice suddenly becomes theirs: stay with honour or leave. She closes her persuasion by weaving together climactically the key thematic words of *Eumenides*, promising they will be 'justly for all time honoured' (891).

Reverence breeds reverence, and the Furies break from their song into speech, joining Athena's discourse with a marked shift in their tenor (892): 'Lady Athena, what seat do you say I would have?' Then a second question, still spoken (894): 'What honour

92

awaits me?' Another eight lines of *stichomythia* dialogue follow, but not, as in previous such exchanges, tense and rapid, but building to the Furies' final question, which asks not what Athena will grant them, but what blessings for this land they will now sing in their hymn (902). This question releases Athena to shift her focus from the Furies back to her city and its citizens, and she closes the trilogy's last spoken lines with the promise to bring honour, not to the Furies, but to the city (915).

Athena has saved first Orestes and then Athens, and, while she thus becomes the first character in the *Oresteia* to escape from the double bind, her divinity is the key to her success. It is critical to understanding the action of *Eumenides* that Athena's intervention has provoked the Furies to this rage because her act, and the Furies' lament, have closed the trajectory of the arc launched by the Watchman's first words at the beginning of the *Agamemnon*: 'I ask the gods for a release from these toils.' The Watchman's prayer refers not just to his endless nights of sleepless, futile anticipation of the signal fires from Troy, but is also programmatic for the entire *Oresteia*. The initial *theous* ('gods') thus prepares and reaches across the roughly 3,500 lines that follow into the Furies' lament, *iô theoi neôteroi* ('o, you young gods', 787/808). Gods, and not humans, have finally delivered release for the House of Atreus, and, indeed, one god, who is completely absent from the *Agamemnon*, thus freeing her from the taint of its vendetta-ridden culture. Not even the post-war storm narrated by the Herald names Athena, a meaningful omission because Aeschylus' audience would have been mindful of Nestor's allusion to Athena's stormy wrath in the *Odyssey* (3.135, 143).[72] That the first line of the *Oresteia* directly connects to its last scene is further indicated by Apollo's instruction at Delphi to Orestes, that he travel to 'the city of Pallas' and claim supplicant status, 'so that you may be released completely from your toils' (83).[73]

The salvation of the House of Atreus relies completely on Pallas Athena's agency. If the human jury had voted to acquit Orestes, whether by virtue of a tie or a majority, then the release would have come as a result of human actions, not divine. But the vote to convict keeps justice squarely in the realm of the blood-driven vendetta system. Humans cannot overcome the dilemma on their own; Athena recognizes the problem and thus she shifts her position from neutral to override the jury's vote and produce the tie that acquits Orestes. It is thus, I suggest, thematically appropriate, if not necessary, that there be an odd number of jurors who elect to convict Orestes of matricide by a single vote, a decision which is then overturned by Athena's ballot. Even if there was an even number of jurors and the vote was tied evenly, Orestes would still need the goddess Athena to announce, after its conclusion, that a draw produces an acquittal.

With Orestes safe, and the Furies now in agreement with Athena, all who stand in the *orchêstra* are now free to sing together, and together for the first time. This joyous song balances, yet builds on, the angry one just after the verdict is announced, as the structure of the exodus again has Athena answering the Furies' song, but now she replies in chanted anapaests instead of spoken iambics. This exchange is yet another transformational echo of *Agamemnon*, the close of which has Clytemnestra answering the chorus in iambics until line 1147, after which she shifts to anapaests. Clytemnestra and the chorus of Argive elders had been competing with one another, but here Athena and the chorus celebrate their new unanimity. The slow, stately lyrics are sung in the lecythion metre, one which had been used briefly in the ode before the trial, yet abandoned for wilder metres as the Furies' anger overtook them again. In the final song of *Eumenides*, the Furies only break off from lecythia to sing in dactyls, the metre of the Homeric epics and hymns.[74] Form matches content, as Athena's actions have been heroic (thus epic), while the Furies are receiving new honours (thus hymn).

The Furies sing their blessings on Athens as they prepare for their new identity, but what this identity is, exactly, is not entirely clear. One would expect Athena to announce that the Erinyes will now be called the Eumenides, 'the fair-minded ones', but, in the text that survives, that does not happen. Many scholars believe that this part of the play was lost in transmission, but the surviving text does present Athena calling them something fairly close to Eumenides: *Euphrones*, the Kindly Ones (992), from whose fearsome faces, the very ones that terrified the Pythia at Delphi, 'I see a great benefit for these citizens' (990-1). In isolation, the idea of beneficial fear sounds paradoxical, but both Furies and Athena individually praise the role of Fear in society (517-25, 698-9). It is, however, also possible that Athena never calls them Eumenides, but Aeschylus' intention was to identify the Furies with the cult of the Semnai Theai, 'the August Goddesses', as she calls them at 1041.[75] The Furies prepare to enter their new home, inside the Acropolis, close to their new host Athena. Cries of *chairete*, first heard from Orestes (or Apollo) as he exited for the last time, are now shared by more, echoed quickly back and forth between Athena and Furies, addressed to each other and to Athens (996, 1003, 1014). This verb can designate both greeting and farewells, but perhaps most significantly here, it also and here primarily says, 'rejoice', an emotion truly felt here, after many false starts, for the first time in the trilogy.[76]

Here the *orchêstra* of the Theatre of Dionysus must have become quite crowded, and spectacularly so, as Aeschylus continues the transfigurations of *Agamemnon*'s themes and images to the final lines of *Eumenides*.[77] The eleven (or ten) jurors have never left, remaining there with Athena, the twelve Furies, and whatever attendants were needed for the trial. As Athena cries her own *chairete*, another group enters from the right, identified by Athena as 'these escorts' (1005), who carry torches, lead sacrificial victims (1006), and bring the purple robes (1027-8) that will physically mark the Furies' transformation into the Eumenides. These new people, the female attendants of the cult of Athena Polias (1024), will sing the final song (1032-47) as a secondary chorus. The presence of sacrificial animals (most likely at least one cow) would signal the end of the threat of improper sacrifice that typified the earlier stages of the House of Atreus. The torches that conduct the Furies to their new home under the Acropolis play off against the destructive signal fires that marked Troy's fall and entered the palace of Agamemnon to feed Clytemnestra's sacrificial fires. The purple (or crimson) robes serve a double function, as they cover the black ones of the Furies. In Athenian terms, the robes mark them as 'metics' (1010, 1018), an official Athenian status of people who were neither citizens nor visitors, but formal permanent residents. They wore their robes especially during the Panathenaic procession. These robes would transform not just the Furies but also the image of the tapestries on which Agamemnon walked in displaying his *hubris* and with which Clytemnestra trapped him fatally, and which Orestes displayed again at the end of *Libation Bearers* before the invisible Furies chased him to Delphi. Sommerstein adds together two torchbearers, Athena, her priestess and attendants, the other servants who brought torches and robes, the herald and trumpeter, the jury members, and the newly robed chorus of Furies/Eumenides and concludes that there must have been roughly 35 people, plus sacrificial animals! But the number is less important than what the combination of its constituent members signifies. The male jury members join with Athena's female attendants in honouring two sets of female (yet sexless) divinities, one Olympian and one Chthonic, thus resolving in one moment the conflicts between genders and classes of gods that marked the entire trilogy. The female attendants' final song closes the trilogy by asking all to 'raise the ritual cry' of joy which was mainly associated with women. In *Agamemnon* it had been raised for the capture of Troy (28, 587, 595) and murder of the king (1118), and then in *Libation Bearers* for his own two murderers in turn (942).[78] A few lines earlier (1038), the women had asked 'the whole city's people', to keep ritual silence and now they bid them sing, all together, in victory. Sommerstein suggests that the entire audience, the true referent of 1038, is thus asked to cry out together, 'as all Athenians hail the birth of a new era'. That, as Laura McClure points out, 'most, if not all of these mouths were male', points to an instability in the final resolution to the problem of the conflict between the sexes that I shall explore in Chapter 6.[79]

5

Justice, Law, and Athenian Politics in *Eumenides*

The preceding discussions have postponed the complexities of *Eumenides'* relationships to the Athenian legal system and to controversies concerning Athenian politics, both domestic and foreign. Greek tragedy tends not to be set in Athens, so *Eumenides* is immediately somewhat unusual, and its focus on the welfare of Athens, coupled with a string of references to places of Athenian interest and problems that were extremely current in the years before the *Oresteia's* production, make it arguably *the* most Athenian of all the surviving Greek tragedies. Aeschylus produced the *Oresteia* shortly after revolutions in Athenian domestic and foreign policies. In 462 BC Athens broke off its alliance with Sparta, which had been championed by the aristocratic general and politician Cimon; Athens then allied with Sparta's enemy Argos. The Athenian Assembly next ostracized Cimon himself as a result of his opposition to the shift.[1] Of the *Oresteia's* three plays, only *Eumenides* bears clear marks of these upheavals. Thus, while references to political strife and an Argive alliance can be explained solely in terms of the play's internal dynamics, one must consider all possibilities in seeing *Eumenides* as a product of its time.[2] In 458 BC, the year of the *Oresteia's* production, there was no more burning question than the role of the Areopagus Council. In this chapter I shall discuss first justice and the Athenian legal system, and the extent to which the trial of Orestes typifies it; then the role of controversies over the reforms of Ephialtes, a few years earlier, which limited the powers of the Areopagus Council established during Orestes' trial; finally, as part of this discussion, I shall examine references in *Eumenides* to the Argive alliance.

Justice in *Eumenides*

Earlier I discussed how Aeschylus' entry into manhood was accompanied by the beginning of Athenian democracy, and how he later defended as a common soldier his city against the Persian threat. His plays participated in the City Dionysia that celebrated, though not uncritically, Athenian greatness. In two other institutions, the Assembly and the courts, the Athenian people regulated their own affairs and made sure civic order was maintained. The two concepts that underlay both institutions were freedom (*eleutheria*) and equality before the law (*isonomia*).[3] With their new freedom came the responsibility to maintain order and lawfulness, and there is no more fundamental aspect of order and lawfulness than restraining oneself from committing murder and from seeking vengeful retribution when murder does occur. *Eumenides* enacts the crisis that happens when vengeance moves inside the family and obliterates the most sacred familial bonds: father and daughter, wife and husband, son and mother. So severe is this crisis that it makes the mysterious divine forces in the universe manifest and participants in its resolution. As almost every commentator on the *Oresteia* has written, justice is *the* great theme of the *Oresteia*, which is largely preoccupied with deciding what, exactly, 'justice' means.

The Greek word for justice, *dikê*, is both simply clear and, at times in the *Oresteia*, dangerously ambiguous.[4] Throughout the *Oresteia*, there are two basic senses of *dikê*, retributive and legal, which are not immediately apparent in English translation. It is used, and used frequently, to denote justice, right, retribution, punishment, law court, and lawsuit. Obviously, these are not all the same things, and their overlapping senses hold the possibility for confusion and manipulation, especially since all characters in the *Oresteia* claim to be concerned with *dikê* or acting for it. The unsuspecting modern reader can easily become even more confused because almost every single word involving justice, the trial and its participants is a *dikê*-related term. The Furies seek *dikê* as retribution while Athena offers *dikê* as trial. *Eumenides* in particular presents a great frequency of *dik-* terms; especially in its second half, the sense of 'legal proceeding' dominates, but its other meanings cannot be simply shut down. *Dikê* seems to involve not merely justice *per se* but a more general sense of proper order. Podlecki observes that *dikê* has a concrete sense of referring 'to the state of affairs which parties who believe they are aggrieved wish to have restored'. In the course of the *Oresteia*, a general sense of redressing wrongs moves to concrete legal or judicial uses: 'It is precisely this field of meaning which enables Aeschylus to bring Justice as an abstract concept or personification into the everyday reality of an Athenian law court.'[5] Aeschylus has in the first two plays carefully prepared his audience for the justice of the trial scene in *Eumenides* by continually casting acts of retribution in metaphors of the courts (e.g. *Agamemnon* 41, 451, 534-5, 1411, 1420-1; *Libation Bearers* 119-20, 987-9).

In *Eumenides* the Furies are upholders of a primordial *dikê*, and their songs indicate that *dikê* entails more than retributive acts, but the order they are intended to restore. Goldhill sums up cogently the centrality of this concept for the *Oresteia*:[6]

'Justice' involves not merely legal order, but the right organization of all the parts and relations of the city. It is in this sense also that one can refer to *dikê* as 'a prime term of social order'. There is more at stake in the complex dynamics of *dikê* in the *Oresteia* than the specific judgment of Orestes' guilt or acquittal.

Indeed, even after Orestes' acquittal *dikê* remains a hotly contested concept and the situation requires another 270 lines for its transformation into the justice of the law court to be fully effected.

This metamorphosis relies on Athena's conversion of the Furies' words. One early exchange (430-3) contains three forms of *dikê* in four lines. Then Athena notes that Orestes had supplicated her statue 'trusting in *dikê*' (439). Orestes asks her to decide the *dikê* whether he acted justly (*dikaiôs*) or not (468). Athena replies with a demurral that she cannot rightly decide such *dikas* (472-3) and then refers to witnesses and evidence as 'sworn safeguards of *dikê*'. The Furies' immediately succeeding song hammers away at the centrality of *dikê* in the universe (490-565), but in terms that Athena strongly echoes shortly afterwards (681-710) when she establishes the tribunal as a permanent fixture for the Athenian people; *dikê* as punishment now becomes *dikê* as court of law. Athena not merely echoes their language but appropriates it for her own purposes. Even after the verdict, Athena continues to adapt the Furies' language, as she begins her persuasion of them (795-6): 'You are not defeated (*nenikêsthe*), but a *dikê* of equal votes has truly resulted not in your dishonour.' Throughout the *Oresteia dikê* as retribution has been accompanied by *nikê*, victory, and the assonance of the two words doubtless added to their association. Athena must remove the zero-sum game of victory and defeat from *dikê* as part of her redefinition of it, if she has any hopes of saving Athens from the Furies' wrath. Once the Furies accept her definition of *dikê*, the word recedes from the celebratory songs and is replaced by terms more concerned with the health of Athens. Whether the problem of defining *dikê* has been resolved at the end remains a matter of scholarly controversy, but, nonetheless, *dikê* as law court has now become in the play's world a reality, not just a metaphor.[7]

Justice in Athens

The trial of Orestes in Aeschylus' *Eumenides* provides a founding charter myth for regulating murder in Athens through the institution of the Areopagus tribunal. Like any myth, Aeschylus' vision condenses and displaces aspects of reality. Let us then look briefly at how Athenian legal mechanisms evolved. This will allow proper consideration, in the next section, of the changes to the Areopagus in the years before the *Oresteia*'s production.

Relatively early, Athens was concerned with regulating murder, but not always through the Areopagus.[8] Around 620 BC an
obscure man named Draco formulated a set of complex laws
that involved a number of subjects, but our sources focus on the
laws regarding homicide, which removed authority over retribution from the family and gave it to the state, and distinguished
between intentional and unintentional killings. That this was a
momentous shift in society is seen by how the popular consciousness was still working out its consequences two centuries later in
such dramas as the *Oresteia* and *Oedipus Tyrannus*. Throughout
Attica there were sanctuaries where the guilty could take refuge
while negotiating recompense with the aggrieved parties. Draco
transferred these responsibilities to the state and established a
more independent judiciary. Draco's homicide laws fail to mention
the Areopagus but identify only ephetes ('referees') as the arbiters
of homicide. Fifth-century Athens divided the authority over
homicide between the Areopagus tribunal and the ephetes. The
Areopagus handled the cases of those guilty of deliberately murdering Athenian citizens, and the ephetes tried the other
murderers. It is likely that the ephetes originally had complete
authority over homicide trials and only later (early in the sixth
century) did Solon give the Areopagus its share.

Athens lacked a police homicide squad and district attorney,
but its administration of justice was nonetheless ornately structured. Murder cases were privately handled and could be
brought to court by anyone, but almost always by the victim's
kin. There were preliminary ceremonies, both ritual and legal,
taking several months, which included oaths taken by prosecutor and defendant while they stood on the severed parts of a
boar and a ram and a bull. Witnesses also swore oaths that
required the destruction of swearer and his house in the event
of perjury. Moreover, witnesses had to swear as to the defendant's innocence or guilt. After the arguments and the
presentation of evidence, judges decided the verdict by ballot,
without discussion. A simple majority of votes could convict and
equality acquitted. The deliberate murderer was punished with
death, the unintentional murderer with exile.

The trial of Orestes in *Eumenides* follows these parameters and offers a credible Athenian proceeding. Of course, typical trials did not feature gods as prosecutors and presiding judges. Clytemnestra lacks kin to prosecute her murderer, so the divine Furies, who embody her wrath, take over the job. In *Eumenides*, the judges swear oaths (483, 680, 710), and Orestes' refusal to swear one is a bone of contention to the Furies (429, 468, 609-15). However, Athenian law would not allow a confessed killer to plead that he had killed 'with justice' or that his crime was forgivable because his victim was a murderer. For dramatic purposes, Aeschylus eschews speeches by the prosecution and defence and presents the trial purely in the form of the cross-examination of the murderer and his witness Apollo through rapid exchanges of single lines. At least half of the jury is not swayed by Apollo's suspect arguments but still recognizes compulsion's role in Orestes' actions. The other half (or just under) sees the urgency in preventing matricide. Athena and jurors thus provide a model for audience members who themselves might serve on such juries. Who, exactly, were the members of the Areopagus jury and how their role evolved are my next subjects.

Aeschylus and the Areopagus

The political divisions of democratic Athens are reflected in the conflicts of Greek tragedy. During the decade before the *Oresteia*'s production, a group of Athenian democrats, led by Ephialtes, attacked two aristocratic bastions that had been resisting further political change: the Areopagus Council and the alliance with Sparta. By 461 BC, Athens had allied itself with Argos, the aristocratic leader Cimon had been ostracized, Ephialtes murdered, and the Areopagus stripped of its political authority. Somehow Athens managed to escape being plunged into civil war. While the Argive alliance was certainly controversial, the reforms to the Areopagus Council were more fundamentally important to Athenian democracy and their role in *Eumenides* harder to decipher, so I shall concentrate my efforts there.

102

5. *Justice, Law, and Athenian Politics in* Eumenides

The Areopagus Council was the oldest deliberative body in Athens, predating by over a century the beginning of democracy in 508. In the seventh century BC it was the most important permanent part of the Athenian government. The requirement for membership was a previous term as an archon, a word that literally means 'leader' or 'ruler'. Nine archons were elected for one-year terms from an exclusive pool of candidates who were of wealthy and well-known families from the top two of the four property classes that Solon had established. These men were the Eupatrids ('of good fathers'). Aeschylus himself was a Eupatrid. The archons governed Athens first alongside just the Areopagus Council and then the popular Assembly. Since the Areopagus membership was composed of former archons, who, after their one-year term, served on the Council for the rest of their lives, the Areopagus could effectively control the archons (Aristotle, *Constitution of Athens* 8). It was, essentially, an elite, closed, and powerful club. The Areopagus' brief was wide-ranging, as it 'had the duty of protecting the laws, and managed the majority and the most important of the city's affairs, with full power to inflict fines and other penalties on all offenders' (8.4). Solon introduced the power of *eisangelia*, whereby any citizen could 'bring in a report' of an alleged crime against the state, and the Areopagus could try and punish the accused (8.4). It also likely provided oversight to magistrates at the end of terms. Such Areopagite duties were ripe for abuse and corruption; Cimon may have used them against his political opponents in the 460s. The Areopagus survived the reforms of the tyrant Peisistratus and the first democrat Cleisthenes, and so by the 460s, after four decades of democracy in Athens, the Areopagus was a retrograde oligarchic body with a power inappropriate to a city that was ostensibly ruled by the people. However, since 486, when the Athenians had begun to select archons by lot, there would have been some dilution of aristocratic dominance. As Ephialtes began to agitate against both Areopagus and Cimon, it seems likely that the former supported the latter.

While the historical sequence is a bit obscure, it seems that Ephialtes first opposed Cimon's pro-Sparta foreign policy and

103

then reformed the Areopagus.[9] Ephialtes led the Assembly in passing measures that severely limited the more expansive older jurisdiction of the Areopagus. Ephialtes stripped the Areopagus of its 'added powers' (*Constitution of Athens* 25.2) by which it wielded 'guardianship and supervision of the state'. He assigned these to the Assembly and people's courts, but he showed his concern for tradition and civic harmony by allowing it to retain its judicial powers, especially over homicide cases. Soon afterwards, some people, presumably angry over the further radicalization of the democracy, assassinated Ephialtes. If they had hoped that the removal of the movement's head would cripple its body, they were wrong, for, around the time of the *Oresteia*'s production, Ephialtes' followers opened the archonship (and thus the Areopagus) to the third of the four Solonian property classes, the Zeugitae, thus continuing the transfer of power to the people. The new leader of the democratic movement was the Eupatrid who, as a young man, had served as the *chorêgos* (financing producer) for Aeschylus the year that he had won with *Persians*: Pericles.[10] This new stage in the ongoing democratic revolution was clearly provoking inner turmoil. It is thus not surprising that at the end of the *Oresteia*, after the young goddess Athena has soothed the anger of the ancient Furies over their loss, she repeatedly inveighs against the evils of internal war, *stasis* (858-66, 976-87).

Just how, exactly, *Eumenides* engages Ephialtes' reforms and what Aeschylus' own opinion was, have been sources of considerable scholarly controversy for the past half-century.[11] Athena establishes the Areopagus tribunal not just for Orestes' trial but also for all time (683-4), and she instructs her people not to make any innovations in the laws governing it (693). Without any knowledge of the last few years of Athenian history, the modern reader would find the institution and instruction fairly easy to understand. But, as the saying goes, a little knowledge is a dangerous thing! Scholars disagree whether Aeschylus was a moderate (the reforms were good, but expansion of the Council to the third class is a bad idea) or a radical (all changes were good, and more would be even better);

a few argue that Aeschylus longs for an oligarchic past.[12] The Argive alliance, the other part of Ephialtes' programme, seems less controversial, as it is spoken of in unreservedly positive terms (289-91, 667-73, 762-74) and validated by being projected back to mythic times. Athena's warnings against meddling in the laws she establishes (693-5) appear especially ambiguous, since the meddling could refer to the powers added to the original judicial role that Athena establishes, or the new reforms themselves. It might then be more productive to heed Schaps' observation that, while the *Oresteia* seems to take clear positions on other matters and pressing political issues, such as the Argive alliance, it also seems to go out of its way to eschew any stance on the contemporary Areopagus; the silence hence must be deliberate. *Eumenides* is thus not a polemical drama, but a patriotic one.[13]

To conclude this chapter, I offer my own take on this problem by returning to the Furies and why Aeschylus involved them in the Areopagus controversy. I suggest that most of these critical readings of *Eumenides* have overvalued its political (in its narrow sense) aspects and undervalued Aeschylus' religious concerns. *Eumenides* concludes neither with Athena's instructions nor the trial of Orestes, but with the transformation of the Furies into the Semnai Theai, 'The August Goddesses' (or the Eumenides). Helen Bacon addressed this matter succinctly in a passage on the culmination of the *Oresteia* in the Furies' installation in Athens that I quoted much earlier (see p. 88).[14] Aeschylus points his audience not at the Areopagus but at the pathology that the Areopagus should punish, homicide, which is precisely the domain of the Furies. The innovative, synthesizing religious imagination of Aeschylus thus sees the disruption of the social order through murder not as a purely human task, but one that humans share jointly with the gods. I return to this joint mission shortly, after a proposal of why Aeschylus involved the Furies in the Areopagus controversy.

Aeschylus, I submit, harnesses the emotional energy generated by the controversies of the previous four years to focus his audience's attention on the larger issue of justice, the *Oresteia*'s

105

main theme. Taking a partisan side in the Ephialtic reforms and their aftermath would have channelled this energy in that direction, while Aeschylus' concern was with the larger issue itself. It is important to keep in mind that the Greek word for justice, *dikē*, involves not just the redressing of injuries but also the natural order. It is a term that, in Aeschylus especially, has cosmic implications. To achieve a world order by justice, humans must work out relations not only among each other, but also between humans and gods. The creation of the Areopagus is an incomplete step on the path to justice without its complementary divine component. Aeschylus knew of the real Areopagus tribunal, he knew of the worship of the Furies and the Semnai in Athens. His masterstroke was to combine them into a single unit: humans working with gods.

But this was not the first time Aeschylus had enacted a drama in which the gods had assisted Athens in the deliverance from a crisis. Fourteen years before the *Oresteia*, Aeschylus' *Persians* depicted an Athens preserved from destruction by the valour of its people and the gods' care against the hubristic Persians. The Messenger who returns from Salamis ends the first part of his report to the Persian Queen with a stress on divine agency (347): 'the gods save the city of the goddess Pallas'. A poet-soldier who had witnessed his people's victory against great odds at both Marathon and Salamis could understandably attribute this success to the cooperative efforts of Athenian soldiers and their Olympian benefactors.

The gods assist the Athenian people in solving their crises and with building a better world. The problem of the vendetta system in the *Oresteia* now solved, Athena can now focus on the productive management of her city. Scholars have long recognized that the parade at the end of *Eumenides*, with the priestess of Athena Polias, female temple attendants, sacrificial animals, Athenian citizens and metics, strongly evokes the Panathenaic procession, the climax of the quadrennial citywide festival in honour of Athena.[15] This scene would be repeated on a temple whose construction began roughly a decade after *Eumenides*, the temple of Athena Parthenos: the

Parthenon. On the temple's inner frieze, high above its floor, relief sculptures depicted the Panathenaic procession, with Athenian citizens, temple attendants, sacrificial animals, and the gods moving casually among the people of Athens. It would certainly be sheer speculation to suggest that Aeschylus' unifying vision at the end of *Eumenides* influenced the team of Phidias, the sculptor of the Parthenon marbles, but one could more safely observe that the co-operative efforts of humans and gods were in the middle of the fifth century an important component of Athenian self-definition. When we worry about the politics of the references to the Areopagus in *Eumenides*, let us not forget that the play's final words belong to the Furies, Athena, and the attendants of her temple (probably!).[16]

6

The Reception of *Eumenides*: Ancient Tragedy, Gender, and the Modern World

Aeschylus' vision of an exonerated Orestes and civic unity at the end of *Eumenides* seems to have been greeted with suspicion, if one considers its echoes in later Greek tragedy, especially Euripides. The modern reception of *Eumenides* has been divided between affirmation of its message and condemnation of its achievement of civic unity at the expense of the suppression of women. This chapter has three components. In the first, I examine the reception of the *Eumenides* in ancient literature; in the second, the modern scholarly battles over gender and their origins in the nineteenth century; and, in the third, *Eumenides* in modern art, literature and performance.

The reception of *Eumenides* in Greek and Roman tragedy

The reception of *Eumenides* in later Greek tragedy involves primarily three areas: further reflections on the Furies themselves, an instantiation of a courtroom drama that involves a member of the House of Atreus, and the moral character of Orestes. All three aspects indicate scepticism towards Aeschylus' solution to the *Oresteia*'s crisis. Because there are so many more surviving tragedies by Euripides (eighteen or nineteen) than by Sophocles (seven), Euripides almost inevitably serves as the fifth century's main commentator on Aeschylean drama, but, nonetheless, his questioning, restless attitude towards his

culture seems to have found a particularly rich mine for inter-
rogation in the *Oresteia*'s conclusion. I shall not here discuss
dramas that reflect primarily on earlier parts of the *Oresteia*,
such as *Iphigenia at Aulis*, but on those that seem to address
Eumenides in particular. These include Euripides' *Electra,
Andromache, Hecuba, Iphigenia at Tauris,* and *Orestes*.[1] Then
I shall briefly consider Sophocles' version of the Furies/
Eumenides in his final work, *Oedipus at Colonus*.

    Electra, Andromache, and *Iphigenia at Tauris* all are par-
ticularly concerned with the relation of Orestes' character to
matricide. *Electra* does engage Aeschylus' *Libation Bearers*
more directly than it does *Eumenides*, but it raises the question
of what kind of son would be willing to kill his mother by
presenting an almost cowardly Orestes who must be bullied by
his sister into killing Clytemnestra (who herself is more sympathetic than in Aeschylus) and who brutally butchers Aegisthus.
At the play's end, just before the Furies chase Orestes from the
stage, the Dioscuri, the divinized brothers of Clytemnestra and
Helen, appear to resolve the moral mess of the homicidal siblings. They criticize the justice of the murders and Apollo's role
(1244-6), and they, not Apollo, instruct Orestes to flee to Athens
and supplicate Athena's statue (1252-7). They also prophesy the
trial at the Areopagus, the split vote and the installation of the
Furies in the Acropolis (1258-75). Euripides thus wraps up
Eumenides in 31 lines, and he seems to move on to the *Oresteia*'s
satyr play *Proteus* with the Dioscuri then telling in six lines
(1278-83) that play's plot: Menelaus' shipwreck in Egypt.
Euripides' playful one-upping of Aeschylus underscores the
brutality of the changed world in which he lives, roughly 43
years after the *Oresteia* and sixteen years after the start of the
Peloponnesian War.

    Another, earlier Euripidean drama of the previous decade,
Andromache, raises further questions of what an Orestes might
be like without the progressive, hopeful schema of Aeschylus.
Orestes appears briefly, but tellingly, in this play. Menelaus
had promised Helen's daughter Hermione to Orestes, but, need-
ing at Troy the help of Achilles' son, Neoptolemus (968-70), he

betrothed her to him. Afterwards, when Orestes asked Neoptolemus to surrender Hermione to him, pleading the difficulty a matricide has in finding a bride, Neoptolemus rejected him derisively (971-8). In vengeance, Orestes arranges for a cowardly murder of Neoptolemus while the latter is on a pilgrimage to Delphi. There is one brief mention of the Furies (978) but none of the trial and Orestes' release. Euripides almost seems to be suggesting, in agreement with the Aeschylean Furies, that it is not psychologically credible that matricide, even involuntary, would not change a man's character. Whom would Orestes not kill again if he saw a chance to gain from the deed?

A vastly different Orestes appears in *Iphigenia at Tauris*, a play that is particularly haunted by the *Oresteia*. Haunted is also the best description for Iphigenia, who has been living on the shore of the Black Sea after Artemis saved her from sacrifice at her father's hands, substituting a deer for her. In other words, the entire *Oresteia*, need not have happened, since Agamemnon did not actually kill Clytemnestra's daughter. Orestes and Pylades arrive, travelling on Apollo's instructions that they must find a special statue of Artemis and bring it to Athens; then his suffering will end, so Apollo says. A splinter group of the Furies, who had rejected the deal with Athena (934-86), continue their pursuit of Orestes and he is described as madly slashing at the air at invisible forces, before falling on a herd of cattle and collapsing in madness (285-305). The Aeschylean Apollo had sworn that Athena and the trial would save him, but the Euripidean Orestes is steadily driven into despair and madness that such a solution turned out to be illusory. The play ends with Athena helping Orestes and Iphigenia to escape Tauris with the statue. Athena insists that she did save him earlier, as the equal votes guaranteed his release (1469-72). Yet she overlooks the Furies' continued pursuit. But have these invisible Furies been real? Is he simply mad?

The madness of Orestes is the focal point of one of Euripides' last tragedies (408 BC), *Orestes*. Like the *Oresteia*, *Orestes* is palpably close to the poet's own time, yet Euripides' dislocations of aspects of his story serve to erode the distancing power of myth that was so important to the success of the end of *Eumenides*. Here Orestes is depraved, almost criminally so, and the court of justice, the matricide's result, already exists and will be used against Orestes even before he reaches Athens, as the Argive Assembly puts him on trial in Argos. This inversion is seconded as the Furies are already called Eumenides (38). Orestes lies feverish in bed, delirious. The Argive assembly will soon vote (46-51, an astonishing anachronism). Apollo seems to have abandoned Orestes, as all characters denounce the god repeatedly, and Menelaus, influenced by Clytemnestra's father Tyndareus, soon turns against him as well. The spectre of mob rule in the Argive assembly, a growing problem in Athens over the previous decade, looms over the play. The Furies remain invisible, but the fury of the Argive people and their armed guards make the goddesses redundant. The mob condemns Orestes and Electra to death – no split decision this time – and Orestes only convinces it not to stone them by offering that he and Electra will commit suicide instead (943-52). Just as the constant drumbeat of pity for Orestes reaches its crescendo, Pylades leads Orestes and Electra to reveal their true natures, as they readily agree to his suggestion that they murder Helen and take Hermione hostage in vengeance (1105-1204). Either matricide has unhinged their moral bearings, or they have been as innately bloodthirsty as their family's previous generations. Redemptive, educational suffering is as far from this world as the Athens of 408 BC is from its version of a half-century earlier. To bring a complex and crazy ending to its climax, Apollo appears with various instructions for the characters, including Orestes' trial at Athens with a divine, not human, jury (1648-52), which suggests that humans have shown that they cannot be trusted with the decision. Orestes will marry, not kill, Hermione, and Helen is now a goddess. This inordinately facile solution to the depravity of the stage world, denying so much of the moral seriousness of *Eumenides*, is strangely appropriate.

Like *Orestes*, the earlier *Hecuba* (around 425 BC) puts a character from the *Oresteia* in a trial and raises questions about

111

the limits of the capacity of the legal system to restrict revenge. *Hecuba* is set immediately following the Trojan War. King Polymestor of Thrace had received Priam and Hecuba's youngest son, along with a considerable supply of gold, to keep both safe from the war. His greed drove him to butcher Polymestor and cast the corpse to the sea. When Hecuba, now Agamemnon's slave, discovers the body, she lures Polymestor and his sons into her tent and, abetted by other Trojan women, kills the boys and blinds Polymestor. The play closes with a trial scene as Agamemnon serves as judge and jury. Hecuba cannot simply take justice into her own hands, but must be held accountable to a third party. The defendant is technically Hecuba, but even Polymestor's prosecution speech sounds more like one given for the defence. After Agamemnon rules in Hecuba's favour, Polymestor prophesies the deaths of Cassandra and Agamemnon by Clytemnestra's axe in Argos (1275-9); in other words, he prophesies the *Oresteia* and, were Agamemnon a bit less clueless, the *Oresteia* might not happen at all! Euripides here collapses together the vendetta system and the legal mechanism that should prevent it, as well as two different stages of the story of Agamemnon's family. As the norms of Greek society crumbled in the Peloponnesian War's early years, Aeschylus' outlook at the *Oresteia*'s end seemed gradually less realistic. By *Orestes* in 408, it was virtually risible.

In the war's final years, Sophocles in turn looked back at the *Oresteia*, though less directly, in his *Oedipus at Colonus*, which was produced after Sophocles' death in 405 and Sparta's defeat of Athens in 404.[2] *Oedipus at Colonus* closes the era that the *Oresteia* began, and in doing so it too evokes the Furies' power and the blessings of the great city of Athens. In the final stage of his wanderings in exile, Oedipus and his daughter Antigone reach the sacred grove of the Eumenides just outside Athens, which he knows will be his ultimate resting place and the site of a tomb through which he, in hero cult, will be able to protect the land, just as Orestes has promised his tomb would for Athens late in *Eumenides*. Unlike the earlier play, the enemy threat is not imagined but real, as the Athens of the audience knows the end of its power is near. Oedipus the patricide complements the matricide Orestes, and in this play he will, essentially, be put on trial to prove, like Orestes, that, while he did kill his parent, he is morally innocent. In both plays, volition is key. Like *Eumenides*, the just city of Athens is contrasted with a corrupt city; here Thebes takes the place of Argos. Oedipus, like Orestes, claims sanctuary, but unlike Orestes he does so at a place sacred to the Furies/Eumenides themselves (44-5). The shape of the action is roughly similar, as a polluted outcast finds sanctuary and a figure associated with anger and vengeance is transformed into something beneficent, but here that figure is not a Fury but Oedipus himself. Yet Oedipus can be transformed here because he deeply resembles the Furies, which Sophocles establishes in detail. Before his transformation into a divinity, Oedipus will display his Fury side against both his brother-in-law Creon, who would drag him back to Thebes and use the power of his tomb against his will, and his son Polynices, who had earlier exiled his father but now needs his blessing for the war against his brother. Oedipus' rage against both is arguably greater than anything seen in the Athenian theatre since Aeschylus' Furies, and at the play's end Oedipus joins the Furies/Eumenides as a Chthonic power. Sophocles, like Aeschylus, is deeply concerned with the relationship between justice, Athens, and the gods. Just as only Athens could institute justice and give a home to the Furies, only Athens can justly receive the homeless Oedipus.[3] Sophocles closes the great eras of Greek tragedy and of Athens itself by returning to the divinities that Aeschylus had installed underneath the Acropolis as part of his vision of a world where violence was limited by the court and by the Furies, and where Athens was blessed and victorious. In doing so perhaps Sophocles hoped that he could stave off the civic dissolution that had threatened Athens around the time of the *Oresteia*'s production a half-century earlier.

The reception history of *Eumenides* now shifts to Rome, and it is not a particularly long history.[4] Ennius wrote a tragedy of this name, which exists now in only a handful of vague fragments. Cicero may have had either Ennius or Aeschylus in mind when he wrote in *Pro Milone* (8) of an Orestes who was 'acquitted by the vote of one who was not merely a goddess, but a goddess pre-eminent for wisdom'. In Vergil's *Aeneid*, the pursuit of Orestes by his mother's spirit is one of the two myths through which the poet tries to describe Dido's sense of terror at her abandonment by Aeneas (4.470-2). The trial of Orestes would await the modern world for further exploration.

The reception of *Eumenides* and the problem of gender

While gender conflicts, begun in the denunciations of Helen and Clytemnestra's 'feminist' rebellion in *Agamemnon*, drive much of the *Oresteia*'s action, commentators on its treatment of women have focused more on *Eumenides* than on the first two plays. Of particular concern have been Apollo's notorious argument in the trial that mothers are not actually blood relatives of their children and the Furies' acquiescence to the new patriarchal order at the trilogy's end. At the close of *Eumenides*, only females are present, yet some scholars see the desexualized Athena and compliant Furies as evidence of a deep-seated misogyny in the *Oresteia*. This section begins with the role of the *Eumenides* in nineteenth-century thought about the status of women before examining Kate Millet's response in *Sexual Politics* and more scholarly considerations of the role of gender and sexuality by such scholars as Foley, Goldhill, McClure and Zeitlin.

Among nineteenth-century intellectuals, and particularly in the German-speaking world that was mad about all things Greek, Aeschylus was enormously popular. Schlegel, Nietzsche and Wagner praised, even worshipped, Aeschylean drama as one of the apexes of Greek civilization, a cultural zenith that was never matched again in originality of conception and execution.[5] But more directly connected to the modern critical reception of *Eumenides* is a book by the Swiss scholar J.J. Bachofen, *Das Mutterrecht* (*The Rule of the Mother*, 1861),

114

which cast a long shadow over subsequent thinking about gender in the *Oresteia*. Bachofen theorized that the society has universally evolved from an original matriarchy to the current patriarchy and that the trial of Orestes in *Eumenides* represents a crucial step in the suppression of women's rights in western civilization. Mankind universally passes through three early stages. The first, 'hetaerism', is characterized by unfettered promiscuity in the worship of Aphrodite. In the second, 'Amazonism', women rebel against their male oppressors. The final stage, 'The Rule of the Mother', ends violently with the establishment of patriarchy. Bachofen immediately influenced Engels and Freud in their writings respectively on the historical development of the family and private property and the individual's turning from mother to father. The gendered terms of social progress in the *Oresteia* remain visible in such diverse texts as Richmond Lattimore's introduction to his translation of the *Oresteia*, which is still widely in use, and George Thomson's Marxist analysis of the trilogy.[6] While modern analysis of the *Oresteia* has long moved away from the myth of an overthrown matriarchy, Bachofen's contention that there is something wrong with *Eumenides* has continued to have influence.

Bachofen's thesis again resonated in the women's movement in the twentieth century. Apollo's words against mothers and Athena's in favour of fathers began to scandalize anew. Most famously (or notoriously), Kate Millet in her *Sexual Politics* decries how Athena 'born full-grown from the head of her father Zeus marches on spoiling to destroy her kind ... this sort of corroboration can be fatal'. The ending of *Eumenides* is not a paean to civic and divine unity, but rather 'five pages of local chamber of commerce rhapsody'. *Eumenides* represents above all the 'triumph of patriarchy'.[7] Millet's feminist polemics are echoed in the English translation of Simone de Beauvoir's *The Second Sex*, published within a year of *Sexual Politics*. But, despite Millet's rejection of Bachofen and Engels, her thought remains within the same evolutionary framework.

To move the discussion forward, scholars would need to see the *Eumenides* not as a reflection of historical reality, but as an

115

expression of fifth-century ideology. In Simon Goldhill's words, which in turn build on the work of Arthur, Pembroke and Vernant: 'The story of rejected matriarchy is the expression of the patriarchal structures of Athenian society.'[8] Thus the male displaces the female as part of a myth that justifies the continuation of male authority in the author's present. Beginning with Winnington-Ingram's 'Clytemnestra and the Vote of Athena' (decades ahead of its time), discussions of how *Eumenides* negotiates its representation of the emergent patriarchal order have formed some of the most stimulating and important work on the *Oresteia*.[9] Because the *Oresteia*'s cycle of revenge alternates murders by a member of one sex against another and culminates in the clash between Apollo and Furies, the problem of revenge is inseparable from gender hierarchies. To quote Goldhill again: 'The seemingly endless pattern of revenge and reversal, then, is also a pattern of male-female opposition, that itself tends towards an opposition of social and political obligations to familial and blood ties'.[10] The escape from the vendetta cycle thus requires some way to surmount gender conflict. Let us look briefly at two relatively recent, representative discussions of gender in *Eumenides*, before turning to examine the pivotal moment in the gender conflicts of the trilogy: Apollo's denial of maternity.

Froma Zeitlin's landmark essay, 'The Dynamics of Misogyny: Myth and Mythmaking in Aeschylus's *Oresteia*', puts women back at the centre of study, positing the *Oresteia*, literally, as a 'gynecocentric (female-centered) document'. Zeitlin focuses on the 'hierarchization of values' in the trilogy. This structure places 'Olympian over Chthonic on the divine level, Greek over barbarian on the cultural level, and male over female on the social level'.[11] The conflict between male and female, however, subsumes the other two polarities and 'sexualizes' them through a central metaphor. The *Oresteia* thus culminates in the re-affirmation of patriarchal marriage and succession. The law court will replace the vendetta, but only by mastering the female. Athena can serve as the mechanism of establishing this control 'precisely because she has no uterine ties of her own and does not herself create one. Free from any but symbolic maternal associations, she thus forswears any matriarchal projects.'[12] One might note here that Zeitlin takes at face value the words of first Apollo and then Athena, but, as we saw earlier and shall again shortly, there are other ways of understanding them. When the Furies agree to work under Athena's aegis, they allow themselves to be redefined and newly limited by the (male) city: 'this last act completes the transference of the *political* power (along the lines of the myth of matriarchy), which Clytemnestra had brazenly claimed in the first play, to the *ritual* power of the female, exemplified by the role now assigned to the Erinyes in Athens'.[13]

This argument is certainly compelling and has been enormously influential since its first publication in the 1970s, but there are two points one could make in response. First, while Athena certainly does identify herself as wholly of the father and deferring to the male in all matters, she does add the important condition 'except for marriage' (737-8). Further, these claims can be read, as argued earlier, as part of a public tactic as she prepares for her negotiations with the Furies. Moreover, her participation in the denial of maternity does not make her masculine; she remains utterly androgynous. Her androgyny is also essential to resolving the crisis. Goldhill notes, 'As the narrative has been structured around the polarized opposition of the genders, so the narrative's ending depends on a figure who does not easily fit into such an opposition.'[14] Indeed, as Winnington-Ingram observed long ago, Athena's very nature destabilizes this tidy ending because she so strongly resembles Clytemnestra: a powerful, persuasive, androgynous being.[15] Second, ritual power is not to be taken lightly. Earlier I noted how scholarship on *Eumenides* that focuses on the importance of the Areopagus winds up neglecting the drama's long ending that has little directly to do with the court but is very much about ritual and religion. Zeitlin's thesis dovetails well with this approach. I wonder to what extent our modern scholarly pre-occupation with politics and the erasure of religion affects such readings.

117

Laura McClure, who focuses on the codes of male and female speech, provides another approach to the problem of the female in *Eumenides*. In *Agamemnon*, Clytemnestra's speech is problematic because it is erotic, androgynous and duplicitous, and directed at a male internal audience. The *Oresteia* moves from Clytemnestra's gendered, sexualized and disruptive language to divinely sanctioned male judicial speech. Athena mediates these two discourses, as the story of her motherless birth from Zeus and her virginity remove feminine guile from her speech. Athena's androgyny becomes central because it desexualizes her and transforms her persuasive power.[16] Earlier I pointed to McClure's objection to Sommerstein's comment on the unanimity of the last line of *Eumenides*. McClure argues instead that 'most, if not all of these mouths were male ... The third play of the *Oresteia* trilogy celebrates the erasure of women's speech from the polis, both in the theatre and in the law court, and further suggests that the only proper speech for women in public, onstage as well as in the polis, is religious.'[17]

Here I return to the text of *Eumenides*, where Apollo deploys his argument against maternity, for this moment generates Athena's final series of moves and the scholarly reception of *Eumenides* that focuses on gender from Bachofen to the present. Earlier I discussed the context of Apollo's final claim, but now let us look at the argument itself, the aim of which is to sever the blood tie between mother and child, rendering her murder not a crime against kinship (657-61):

I'll also tell you this, and learn how rightly I shall speak:
The so-called mother is not the child's
begetter, but a nurse of a newly sown embryo;
The one who mounts begets, but she, like a stranger to a
    stranger,
preserves the seedling, unless some god harms it.

The phrase 'stranger to a stranger' requires some examination, which will occur shortly.

The most pressing issues are the origins of this thought and its credibility.[18] First, Aeschylus did not invent this idea. Aristotle (*Generation of Animals* 736b31-3) attributes it to Anaxagoras, whose work and even self Aeschylus could have known. Educated Athenians in the audience could have well been acquainted with this theory of reproduction, but it is highly unlikely that the average Athenian (let alone the educated one) would have accepted it, for he was typically deeply prejudiced against natural philosophy, as a mere glance at Socrates' protestations against being considered an advocate in Plato's *Apology* shows (26d-e). In the 430s there was even a decree in the Athenian Assembly against Anaxagoras (Plutarch, *Pericles* 32). Apollo's use of this argument thus would have contributed to the more general impression of sophistry on his part. Further, the emotional power of motherhood throughout Greek myth, seen in such stories as the cosmic grief of Demeter over her lost daughter Persephone, suggests that such a simple argument, even if seized on by Athena, would not be compelling. Last, we should be guided by the vote of the Areopagites, at least half of whom do not accept what Apollo says and vote to convict. But Athena, who has seemed partial to Orestes since her first words in the play, jumps on the argument as a way to exonerate Orestes, since her own birth provides such an easy proof.

To close this section, I return to the uninformative English phrase 'like a stranger to a stranger', for it is richer and more complex than Apollo allows. The Greek is *xenôi xenê*, which is best, if cumbersomely, translated, 'a female guest-friend to a male guest-friend', and thus points us to the guest-host relationship (*xenia*), the ritualized friendship that was so important to early Greek social bonds. In the polarities of the *Oresteia*'s conceptual matrix, *xenia* as culture is male, while blood ties as nature are female. *Xenia* has been a constant theme from the start of the *Oresteia*, as, for example, Zeus Xenios, Zeus of Guest-friendship, sends Menelaus and Agamemnon to Troy for Paris' sins against this code (*Agamemnon* 362). As Bacon observes, 'all the outrages of the *Oresteia* are also involved with the relations of host and guest'.[19] The Furies themselves begin

Eumenides as wandering strangers whom Athena receives as host into her 'house', Athens. When Orestes gained entry to the palace through deception in order to commit murder, he violated both his blood relationship with his mother and the bond of *xenia*. Such passages set the stage for designating maternity as *xenia* in a way that upends the trilogy's gender discourses. While most scholarship has seen the dissolution of the mother's blood tie to child as a denigration of the female, the recasting of maternity in terms of *xenia* actually elevates it according to the *Oresteia*'s conceptual structure. Bacon continues, 'In a surprising inversion Aeschylus represents the female role as that of culture, *xenia* ... The male engenders like an animal; the female nurtures with her skills.'[20] The female is not passive nature, but active culture. I suggest that Apollo intends the stricter simple meeting of 'stranger', but the trilogy's larger network of associations expands its meaning into its larger cultural role of 'guest-friend', and that sense is what Athena hears. Athena is a virgin goddess who will never be a mother, but she is also a goddess of craftsmanship, so this would be an argument with which she has some kind of personal connection.

Placed in its broader cultural contexts, this passage is remarkably rich and multi-faceted, but its speaker's nature and its potentially incendiary content frequently obscure our understanding of these contexts. As noted before, only the androgynous Athena is able to fashion an escape from the *Oresteia*'s gender-driven vendettas, and in her support for Orestes she grabs hold of the seemingly simple and dubious line that Apollo floats in her direction. The *Oresteia* here newly insists on the role of cultural laws, as opposed to blood ties, but it does so in a way that escapes the binary oppositions between male-culture and female-nature. The Furies in their new role will oversee these laws and their institutions. At this point I end my discussion of gender in *Eumenides*, but I have little doubt that the history of the reception of this subject will not end any time soon.

Eumenides and modern culture

The story of Orestes and the Furies has resonated in modernity in multiple ways. We have already seen how Athena's decision to side with the male against the female has produced consternation among feminist authors. In this section I shall discuss the Furies' incarnation in modern art and literature, and the history of performance of Aeschylus' *Eumenides* from the nineteenth century onwards. Unlike some Greek myths, the story of Orestes does not have a continuous reception history after classical antiquity, but becomes of sustained interest only late in the nineteenth century.

Much of the early recreation of the *Oresteia* and thus *Eumenides* occured in France. Voltaire composed *Oreste* in 1761. The elder Dumas translated the *Oresteia* into French in 1856, which then likely spawned *Les Erinnyes*, a play by Leconte de Lisle with music by the opera composer Jules Massenet; despite its title, this play's content corresponds to the first two parts of Aeschylus' trilogy. In 1920 the poet Paul Claudel concluded his translation of the *Oresteia*, with incidental music by Darius Milhaud.

Opera itself figures prominently into the reception history of *Eumenides*. Given that one of Richard Wagner's main inspirations for his *Ring* was the *Oresteia*, further operatic versions of Aeschylus' story should not come as a surprise. In 1895, the Russian Sergei Taneyev composed his own Oresteian trilogy. This was followed by an operatic trilogy by, appropriately enough, the great Wagnerian conductor Felix Weingartner in 1902 and then the Austrian Ernst Krenek's single opera in five acts *Leben des Orest* (*Life of Orestes*) in 1929. During 1965-6 the Greek composer Xenakis composed his own *Oresteia* for two choruses (one of them children) and chamber ensemble.[21] Last, in 2006 a new opera by composer Andrew Earle Simpson and librettist Sarah Brown Ferrario, *The Furies*, based directly on Aeschylus, received its premiere in Washington, DC.

The pursuit of Orestes by the Furies has proved a powerful subject in modern art. The earliest known version is, strangely

121

enough, a humorous cartoon by Alexander Runciman (1736-1785), now in the National Galleries of Scotland. The French painter Bourguereau in 1862 represented the young Orestes (naked as in an ancient vase painting), turning from his dying mother with the angry Furies immediately hounding him. A monumental painting by the American John Singer Sargent (1856-1925), now in the Boston Museum of Fine Arts, shows a more nightmarish vision of Bourguereau, with the naked Orestes fleeing Furies who carry snakes in their right hands, which thrust at the frantic Orestes, and torches in their left. Clytemnestra stands close to Orestes, in bloody garments, glaring at him. All seem to float in the air before a bloody purple background.[22]

Three giants of twentieth-century literature contributed theatrical recreations of *Eumenides*, with varying degrees of success. In Eugene O'Neill's 1931 trilogy, which was set in New England after the Civil War, *Mourning Becomes Electra*, the final play, *The Haunted*, depicts the struggles of a modern Orestes, Orin, to deal with the consequences of the murder of his mother. The Furies do not appear, but they are internalized in the form of Orin's descent into madness. Soon after O'Neill, T.S. Eliot wrote his single play, *The Family Reunion*, which was very loosely based on Aeschylus. Eliot also depicts a haunted young man, Harry, who returns home from a form of exile to his ancestral home in the north of England. Harry is haunted by the death of his wife and fears he may have caused it. Unlike O'Neill, Eliot had the Furies appear onstage, all through the play's first part, but as unspeaking characters; Eliot's stage directions call them not Furies but Eumenides. The effect has never been particularly great theatre, and Eliot later wrote of his regrets at his decision to make them visible.[23] In the second part of the play, Harry learns that these figures are in fact 'Well-Wishers', a loose translation of 'Eumenides'.

In 1942, while the Nazis occupied Paris, the French Existentialist philosopher Jean Paul Sartre wrote his play, *Les Mouches* (*The Flies*). In Jean Girardoux's *Electra* of 1938 one character refers to the Eumenides buzzing like flies, which

becomes the starting point for Sartre's work. His version of the
Orestes story certainly seemed to its audience to bear a remarkable resemblance to the moral dilemmas resented by the Nazi
Occupation. A swarm of huge malodorous flies and avenging
spirits plague the city of Argos. Orestes returns to the plague-
ridden city of his birth, feeling a need to return home to join his
people in their suffering. He kills Aegisthus, who has been a
usurper oppressing the people like the Nazis, and his mother,
who would be seen as a collaborator, like the Vichy government.
In the play's final act the Furies appear as characters, and his
ruined sister Electra offers herself to them. Just as they are
about to destroy her, Zeus appears and gives the siblings the
chance to repent for their mother's murder (which would, in
Sartre's existentialism, destroy them as autonomous human
agents). Orestes rejects Zeus, while Electra, horrified, concedes,
a gesture that allows the Furies to focus on her brother. The
play ends with Orestes' revelation of himself as king and scape-
goat for the collective sins of Argos; he flees, and the Furies
pursue. The play is clearly a mixture of the second two parts of
Aeschylus' trilogy, with Zeus taking over the role of Athena, but
with the twist that this god would deny the existential self-
actualization of the hero, not liberate him. This Orestes discovers
that the gods are not just. I might add here a reminder that
Sartre's partner, Simone de Beauvoir, later found different uses
for Aeschylus in her denunciation of Athena's choice in *The
Second Sex*. *The Flies* has fared perhaps best of the modern
versions, with regular new stagings.

I close with the modern performance history of *Eumenides*, a
history of not particularly great substance, but with one note-
worthy aspect. While productions of Greek tragedy have
increased in frequency, a theatre company bold enough to stage
Aeschylus almost invariably chooses the more widely known
Agamemnon over its successors.[24] A full list of productions of
Eumenides appears in the Chronology that follows this chapter.
According to the APGRD database (Archive of Performances of
Greek and Roman Drama), between 1885 and 2005 there were
26 productions of *Eumenides* (as opposed to the complete *Or-*

esteia). Strangely enough, four of these were clustered between 1885 and 1901, fairly early in the history of modern staging of ancient drama. In 1885, one of the very first of the annual Greek plays at Cambridge University was not *Agamemnon* but *Eumenides*, in a production with music by Stanford.[25] In the succeeding three years there were three separate productions of *Eumenides*, and in 1901 *Eumenides* inaugurated the new Greek theatre in Point Loma, California. In 1907 the Cambridge production was brought to the University of California, Berkeley. The relative popularity of *Eumenides* at this time likely stems from its optimistic content. The Furies might be scary for a while, but everything works out in the end! No incest, no patricide, no civil wars. Moreover, Aeschylus' paeans to progress, enlightenment and nationhood certainly must have sat well with the customs and beliefs of the Victorian era in Britain and America. A culture more under the influence of feminism would later find the rebellion of Clytemnestra in *Agamemnon* a more satisfying theatrical experience, and the Furies' acquiescence at the trilogy's end more objectionable.

Notes

Full bibliographical details of works referred to by short titles in the Notes are to be found in the Bibliography

1. Aeschylus the Athenian

1. For a productively sceptical look at the ancient biographies of Greek poets, see Lefkowitz, *Lives*.

2. Henderson, 'Women', argues for the limited presence of women in the Athenian theatre, as do Csapo and Slater, *Context*, 286-7. For the opposite view, see Goldhill, 'Language'.

3. For introductions to Cleisthenes and Athenian democracy, from a range of perspectives, see the essays in Rhodes, *Athenian Democracy*.

4. Excellent brief overviews of the life of Aeschylus and his place in Athens and early theatre include Herington, *Aeschylus*, 15-31; Winnington-Ingram, 'Aeschylus'; and Goldhill, *Aeschylus*, 1-19.

5. On the battle of Salamis and Aeschylus' *Persians*, see Rosenbloom's excellent account in this same Duckworth series.

6. See Hall, *Inventing*.

7. See 288, 345, 417, 463-507.

8. On Amazons as Persians, see duBois, *Centaurs*, especially 54-7 and 67-8, and Tyrrell, *Amazons* 49-52 and 60-3.

9. On the Odeion see Wiles, *Tragedy*, 54-7. Plutarch, *Pericles* 13.9 attests to the Persian symbolism of the roof.

10. Against the Aeschylean authorship of *Prometheus Bound*, see West, 'Prometheus', and in favour of it, Herington, *Aeschylus*, 157-77 and Saïd, 'Aeschylean Tragedy', 216.

11. Gantz, 'Aischylean Tetralogy', provides a detailed overview of this subject. One should allow that a Promethean trilogy is almost as debated as much as its Aeschylean authorship. In the introduction to his new Loeb edition, Sommerstein now argues that *Persians* was part of a trilogy, as its earlier parts anticipated through myth the historical events of *Persians*.

12. Griffith, 'Slaves' discusses the relationship between *Proteus* and the *Oresteia*.

13. Gantz, 'Aischylean Tetralogy'.

14. I discuss the effect of Cassandra's surprising speech in 'Marriage', building on the earlier work of Knox, 'Aeschylus'.

2. *Eumenides* and Greek Myth and Religion

1. The most useful starting point for the myths of *Eumenides* is Gantz, *Early Greek Myth*, 676-86. For specialized, detailed treatments of the myths behind *Eumenides*, see Sommerstein, *Aeschylus: Eumenides*, 1-12; and Podlecki, *Aeschylus: Eumenides*, 1-9. Those especially interested in the Furies should consult first Bacon, 'Furies' and Johnston, *Restless*, 250-87, and then Brown, 'Eumenides' and 'Erinyes'.

2. On the Homeric suppression of intra-familial violence, see Seaford, *Ritual*.

3. In addition to Herodotus 1.67-8, Pausanias reports tombs of Orestes at Tegea (8.54.4) and Sparta (3.11.10); these two accounts match with Herodotus' story of the bones being moved from Tegea to Sparta. Neither place is located remotely close to the roads from Argos to Athens, and only the ground where the hero was buried could offer assistance.

4. Thus, Sommerstein, *Aeschylus: Eumenides*, 4-6.

5. Euripides, *Orestes* 1650-2. See also Demosthenes 23.66 in the fourth century, who cites 'the twelve gods'. I must wonder whether the Euripidean Apollo's promise of a divine jury to Orestes, in a play a half-century after the *Oresteia*, is a Euripidean joke, somewhat along the lines of Achilles' threats in the nearly contemporaneous *Iphigenia at Aulis* to go home even before the Trojan War starts.

6. Podlecki, *Aeschylus: Eumenides*, 7.

7. Sommerstein (*Aeschylus: Eumenides*, 11-12) summarizes the arguments, as does Podlecki, *Aeschylus: Eumenides* 6-7. For a more detailed view of the role (if any) of the missing lines, and an overview of the problem of the term 'Eumenides', see Brown, 'Eumenides'.

8. Lattimore's introduction (*Aeschylus*, 29) fudges the issue without much explanation with 'The Furies' in a parenthesis after the section head 'Eumenides'.

9. On the Semnai and suppliant protections see Plutarch, *Solon* 12.1; Thucydides 1.126.11; Aristophanes, *Knights* 1312; Aristophanes, *Thesmophoriazousae* 224.

10. See Johnston, *Restless*, 250-88.

11. On the role of Aeschylus' dramatic needs in the shaping of his Furies, see Brown, 'Erinyes', especially 26.

12. On Hesiod, cosmogonic myth, and Aeschylus, see Rabinowitz, 'From Force to Persuasion'. Solmsen, *Hesiod and Aeschylus* is also useful here.

13. On Chthonic religion in Greece, see Burkert, *Greek Religion*, 190-208. Burkert is an excellent introduction to the Olympians as well.

14. Burkert, *Greek Religion*, 202.

15. Bacon, 'Furies', 51.

16. So argues Bacon, 'Furies', 50. Solmsen (*Hesiod and Aeschylus*, 186-9) early argued that the Furies are servants of the Moirai, not Zeus. On this topic see also Winnington-Ingram, *Studies*, 154-74, and Brown, 'Erinyes', 13-34.

17. On the relationship between the *Hymn to Apollo* and the opening of *Eumenides* see Zeitlin, 'Dynamics', 100-4 and Rabinowitz, 'From Force to Persuasion', 78-84.

18. On these versions and their role in Athenian myth and ideology, see Tyrrell and Brown, *Athenian*, 180-1. Zeitlin ('Dynamics', 115-18) considers these myths in relation to the *Oresteia*.

19. Bacon, 'Furies', 57.

3. The Theatre of Aeschylus

1. For evidence for the early Theatre of Dionysus and the Dionysia, see Csapo and Slater, *Context*. The touchstone for any discussion of Aeschylus and the theatre remains Taplin, *Stagecraft*, which expressed very strong views on virtually every aspect of its topic. Taplin can now be supplemented by Hammond, 'Conditions' and 'More on Conditions'; Sider, 'Stagecraft'; Wiles, *Tragedy*, and Ley, *Theatricality*. Gould, 'Tragedy', provides a brief and lucid introduction to Greek theatrical performance.

2. The shape of the orchestra has been disputed. On the evidence and an argument for the circle, see Wiles, *Tragedy*, ch. 2, 'The Theatre of Dionysus', and Scullion, *Three Studies*, ch. 1, 'The Fifth-Century Theatre of Dionysos'. This position is also supported by Ley, *Theatricality*, x-xi.

3. For a brief but very informative and clear account of the beginning of Greek tragedy, see Winnington-Ingram, 'Origins'.

4. Essential reading on the City Dionysia and Athens: Easterling, 'A Show'; Goldhill, 'The Audience of Greek Tragedy'; and Goldhill, 'Great Dionysia'.

5. On this revolution, see Herington, *Poetry into Drama*.

6. On the earliest performance spaces, see in particular Hammond, 'Conditions'.

7. Hammond ('Conditions', 413) provides a useful reminder that a fragment of Aristotle in Themistius attributes the introduction of the third actor to Aeschylus, not Sophocles, and thus this matter must have been in dispute during the fourth century.

8. Csapo, 'The Men', presents the available evidence on the wooden benches and the size of the theatre.

9. Hammond ('Conditions', 406-29) argues for the presence of the rock and its role in the *Oresteia*. Taplin (*Stagecraft*, 448-9) argues against Hammond's thesis, but Taplin is himself rebutted, quite compellingly, by West. 'Prometheus Trilogy', 135-6. Hammond offers his own rebuttal in 'More on Conditions', 23. Wiles (*Tragedy*, 65) agrees with Taplin.

10. Uould, ('Performance') presents the argument for the acoustics of the Athenian theatre requiring a stage as a sounding board. Wiles (*Tragedy*, 65) points out that performances in the Epidaurus theatre were without a temporary stage house, but Wiles neglects that the acoustics of the planned stone Epidaurus *theatron* would have been far superior to the more ad hoc conditions on the Athenian Acropolis. Hammond ('Conditions', 414) reckons the Aeschylean stage was 18 metres in length. Sommerstein (*Aeschylus: Eumenides*, 33), however, observes, 'Nothing in the *Oresteia* clearly indicates whether there was yet a raised platform in the front of the *skene.*'

11. Taplin, *Stagecraft*, 365-74, argues Aeschylus did not use this device.

12. Ley, *Theatricality*, 40-1.

13. Hammond, 'Conditions', 440-1. Sommerstein (*Aeschylus: Eumenides*, 32 n. 104) says this suggestion is 'unacceptable' because trial is held *on* Areopagus, not adjacent, and, in the theatre, the trial is next to the rock, in the *orchêstra* itself. This objection to a simple gesture strikes me as too literal, and analogous to complaining about the verisimilitude of the rapid progress of the signal fires across the Aegean in *Agamemnon*.

14. On the *Agamemnon skênê* as belonging to Apollo, see my article, 'Marriage', 285-8.

15. On the dozen members in the chorus of the *Oresteia*, see Hammond, 'Conditions', 418-19. Taplin (*Stagecraft*, 323 n. 315) argued for fifteen, but most now believe the number was twelve.

16. Marshall, 'Casting', 258. Marshall's work is highly recommended to anyone interested in the number of actors and how parts were distributed.

17. Marshall, 'Casting', 260.

18. Sommerstein, *Aeschylus: Eumenides*, 80.

19. Belfiore, *Tragic*, 20-2.

4. The Play and its Staging

1. Wiles, *Tragedy*.

2. Hammond, 'Conditions', 439 n. 95.

3. Taplin, *Stagecraft*, 362-4, against the *ekkylêma*. See also, Hammond, 'More on Conditions', 49.

4. Taplin, *Stagecraft*, 365-74, Hammond, 'Conditions', 439; Hammond, 'More on Conditions', 26-7; Sommerstein, *Aeschylus: Eumenides*, 93-4; Podlecki, *Aeschylus: Eumenides*, 12-13; Ley, *Theatricality*, 42-4. Hammond ('Conditions', 439) argues for a very awkward scenario of Orestes, Furies and *omphalos* stone moving from *ekkyklêma* to *orchêstra* after the acting area has emptied of actors. My general discussion here assumes that Sommerstein is correct in his commentary (93-4, on lines 85-7 and 64) that lines 85-7 make much more sense as the first words in this exchange and have been transposed from their traditional place after Apollo's first speech. Both Brown ('Some Problems', 29) and Sommerstein argue for the *ekkyklêma*'s use here. Among the modern translations of the *Oresteia*, only Collard's incorporates this emended reading of the line order.

5. Brown 'Some Problems', 28; Podlecki, *Aeschylus: Eumenides,* 12.

6. On the back of the *ekkyklêma*: Sommerstein, 9; above the temple on the roof of the *skênê*: Brown, 'Some Problems', 29, and Wiles, *Tragedy*, 180. Meineck's translation suggests that Apollo *could* be on the roof for his second appearance.

7. See Taplin, *Stagecraft*, 364-5 against Hermes' presence. In response, Brown ('Some Problems', 30) is a bit more sensitive to the play's language here, which he suggests indicates that Apollo turns to Hermes, and leaves the matter an open question. Hammond ('More on Conditions', 27) produced *Eumenides* and found 'no difficulty' with Hermes' presence.

8. On the metaphor of the hunt in the *Oresteia*, see Vidal-Naquet, 'Hunting' and Lebeck, *Oresteia*, 63-8.

9. Scott, *Musical Design*, 113. See further his important discussion, 113-22, on the musical form, or formlessness, of the Furies' entrance song.

10. So Taplin, *Stagecraft*, 372.

11. Rabinowitz ('From Force to Persuasion', 74-8) discusses *Eumenides*' evocations of the *Hymn to Apollo* in the context of a larger study of the role of cosmogonic myth in the *Oresteia*.

12. On the importance of suppliancy in Greek culture, see John Gould's classic essay, '*Hiketeia*', 22-77 in Gould, *Myth*.

13. Wiles (*Tragedy*, 83) argues that the statue of Athena was placed in the centre of the orchestra at the beginning of *Eumenides*.

14. In his translation Meineck has Athena enter through the doors, arguing in his note on line 398 that since 'the scene building has been established as Athena's temple in Athens, it would seem logical that the goddess would enter via the doors'. While he acknowledges that others propose her entrance from the side or above, he does not mention that they argue thus because she is clearly coming from Troy.

15. Taplin (*Stagecraft*, 377-9, 390-1) discusses the settings and the handling of time in detail.

16. Taplin, *Greek Tragedy in Action*.

17. Taplin (*Stagecraft*, 386 n. 1), Rehm ('Staging', 102), Ewans (*Oresteia*, 210) and Wiles (*Tragedy*, 83) argue the statue of Athena must be at the centre so that the Furies can dance around Orestes in the Binding Song. Wiles' argument is part of his larger thesis that the *orchêstra*, not the stage, was the primary acting area. Taplin is remarkably uninterested in this aspect of staging. On the other hand, Sommerstein (*Aeschylus: Eumenides*, 133-4) notes that nothing in the Binding Song necessitates that the Furies surround Orestes. Podlecki (*Aeschylus: Eumenides*, 13-14) will not decide on a place based on the available evidence, and Ley (*Theatricality*, 42-3) has doubts about the importance of the matter, despite sharing Wiles' belief in the significance of the *orchêstra* as an acting space.

18. Burkert, *Greek Religion*, 80-2.

19. Zeitlin, 'Dynamics', 104-6.

20. For fuller discussions of the nature of Orestes' pollution and the ambiguities over the extent of his ritual cleansing see Taplin, *Stagecraft*, 381-4 and Parker, *Miasma*, 386-8.

21. Scott, *Musical Design*, 114. Scott 113-18 is extremely helpful in showing the chaos out of which the final order of *Eumenides* emerges. Scott's comments (118) on the relationship between metre, content and movement in 254-63 are worth quoting in full: 'The Furies sing random lines containing no particular pattern and are free to move as individuals in the orchestra ... They search out their victim and then close in on him as separate entities rather than as members of an organized chorus who must always be conscious of the group nature of their dance.'

22. On the important theme corrupted sacrifices in the *Oresteia*, Zeitlin, 'Motif', remains essential reading.

23. See the commentaries of Sommerstein 136-7 and Podlecki 156, who quotes private correspondence with Stanley Ireland that the anapaests would suggest their 'coming into formation around their victim with almost military precision'.

24. On the location of the statue of Athena see above, n. 17. Sommerstein (*Aeschylus: Eumenides*, 123-4) argues that, if the statue is near the *skênê*, it can easily fade into the background when no longer relevant to the action or be withdrawn quickly on the *ekkyklêma*. On the other hand, Sommerstein himself observes of the preparations for the trial scene (185) that stage hands must have appeared with the juridical paraphernalia, and these same agents could have carried off the statue while bringing on the props.

25. Faraone, 'Aeschylus' ὕμνος δέσμιος', 150. Faraone's starting point is the contention of Lebeck (*Oresteia*, 150) that the chorus' actual stress on Apollo's conduct renders the title 'Binding Song' irrelevant.

26. Taplin (*Stagecraft*, 75-8, 200-2, 388-90) argues against arrival by chariot as the invention of later Hellenistic producers who loved spectacular entries. He also excludes arrival by *mêchanê*. Sommerstein (*Aeschylus: Eumenides*, 153) supports Taplin against the chariot but allows that *mêchanê* would have been available at this point in Aeschylus' career and points out that 403-4 implies continuous motion over land and sea, which would be possible only by air. I think that such thinking involves far too much naturalism in the conception of staging. Podlecki (*Aeschylus: Eumenides*, 164) makes a compelling case for the chariot, based on a reading of the manuscript inconsistencies, and this position has more recently argued by Himmelhoch ('Athena's Entrance'), I believe conclusively, based on the manuscript reading, the themes of the *Oresteia*, and patterns in staging. I weigh in on this topic in my recent article, 'Marriage', 291-2. I add here that the verb in 404, *rhoibdousa*, indicates sound, not motion, and it remains possible that 404 and 405 are not incompatible.

27. See Mitchell-Boyask, 'Marriage.'

28. Himmelhoch, 'Athena's Entrance', 294.

29. Podlecki (*Aeschylus: Eumenides*, 166) observes: 'The notion of reverence (*sebas*) plays a large part in the Erinyes' thinking (vv. 151, 535, 545, 715)'. See also Vellacott, 'Has Good Prevailed?', on the centrality of reverence.

30. Sommerstein (*Aeschylus: Eumenides*) notes: 'but only after his acquittal will he become Argive again in the full sense, able to enter into his own inheritance and to take part in the full civic and religious activities of his *polis*'.

31. Griffith, 'Brilliant Dynasts', 100. While I think that Griffith implies too much that the outcome of the trial is predetermined by these aristocratic alliances, his focus on the class associations of the various figures in the *Oresteia* is extremely valuable.

32. Podlecki's shrewd observation on the difference between Athena and the other Oresteian deities (*Aeschylus: Eumenides*, 168) is worth quoting here: 'Unlike her half-siblings Artemis in *Ag.* and Apollo in *Cho.* Athena refuses to fall too easily into partisanship or favoritism.'

33. Readers who encounter *Eumenides* only in translation are unlikely to know the lightning metaphor is present; in the many translations of the *Oresteia* sitting in my office, only Podlecki translates the verb with its full potential. The same verb is used for Zeus' punishment of the Persians in Aeschylus (*Persians*, 514), and in Sophocles of the plague that strikes *Thebes* by the will of the gods (*Oedipus Tyrannus*, 28), as well as the lightning bolt Heracles hopes his father will send to end his life (*Trachiniae* 1087). I discuss these passages, in the context of Thucydides' use of the verb in his plague narrative (2.47.3), in *Plague*, 85-6.

34. Hammond ('Conditions', 441 n. 97) speculates that if Athena had entered by chariot then 'the chariot leaves at line 489; and it may have been the need to get it off which prompted Aeschylus to make Athena go and fetch the citizens rather than send for them'.

35. There is some ambiguity as to whether she selects the best in order to decide, or she will return in order to decide (after selecting them). I believe it is more the latter, though the ambiguity itself suggests a joint decision.

36. Scott, *Musical Design*, 125-7. See also Chiasson, 'Lecythia'.

37. On the scene change (or not), Orestes' presence, and other matters of staging here, see Taplin, *Stagecraft*, 100-2; Ley, *Theatricality*, 42-4; Hammond, 'Conditions', 440-1 and 'More on Conditions', 27-9; Podlecki, *Aeschylus: Eumenides*, 14-16; Sommerstein, *Aeschylus: Eumenides*, 184-5.

38. Hammond, 'Conditions', 441, citing lines 884, 888, 890, 902, 912, 927, 978, and 991 as configuring the *orchêstra* as Athens.

39. Hammond, 'Conditions', 441.

40. Pickard-Cambridge (*Dramatic*, 46) puts the jury in front of Athena, but Wiles (*Tragedy*, 211) answers that such a position would make it 'impossible acoustically for Athene to turn her back on the *theatron*, and words notionally intended for the jurors have to be addressed in the direction of the audience'.

41. Ley, *Theatricality*, 44-5.

42. Sommerstein comments (*Aeschylus: Eumenides*, 189): 'This is Athena's city and Athena's court: Apollo is subordinate, and Athena at once puts him firmly in his place'.

43. Meineck (*Aeschylus: Oresteia*, 141, note on 574) observes: 'It is difficult to pin down Apollo's movements in this scene. His sudden entrance and departure work well on the roof of the scene building, which also creates a spatial opposition between the Chthonic Furies in the orchestra and the Olympian Apollo high on the roof. It would be appropriate for Athena as mediator to be on stage in the central position'.

44. Taplin, *Stagecraft*, 394.

45. Taplin (*Stagecraft*, 129-34) argues against audience involvement. Sommerstein's contrary thesis (*Aeschylus: Eumenides*, 186) seems judicious and compelling. More recently, Wiles (*Tragedy*) devotes a chapter ('*Orchêstra* and *theatron*', 207-21) to explore the exploitation of the *theatron* space and audience by Greek tragedians; see 211-12 on *Eumenides* in particular, where he supports Sommerstein. Belfiore (*Tragic Pleasures*, 26-8) explores the emotional impact of this involvement.

46. For the myth of the destruction of Asclepius, see Pindar, *Pythian* 3, and the opening of Euripides' *Alcestis*.

47. Sommerstein (*Aeschylus: Eumenides*, 208). His discussion of this entire argument (206-9) is essential reading for anyone interested in Apollo's argument.

48. See Bacon ('Furies', 55-7) on the importance of the word *xenos* in this passage, and below, Chapter 6.

49. See Gagarin, 'Vote'; Hester, 'Casting Vote'; Seaford, 'Historiciz-ing Tagic Ambivalence'; and Winnington-Ingram, 'Clytemnestra', in *Studies*.

50. Sommerstein, *Aeschylus: Eumenides,* 221-6.

51. Podlecki, *Aeschylus: Eumenides*, 182. In general on this pas-sage, Sommerstein's comments (*Aeschylus: Eumenides*, 229-31) are extremely helpful.

52. Fraenkel, *Aeschylus: Agamemnon*, II 376 at ll. 816ff.

53. Douris, Vienna 3695 and the Painter of the Louvre G265. Both of these can be seen in Boegehold, 'Signifying Gesture'.

54. Sommerstein, *Aeschylus: Eumenides* , 221

55. I must acknowledge here that the identity of the speakers of 748-51 is contested. Podlecki's edition gives 748-9 to the chorus and 750-1 to Orestes. Sommerstein (*Aeschylus: Eumenides*, 233), whom I follow here, is certain lines 750-1 are spoken by Apollo. Glenn Most has recently suggested that 775-7 belong to Apollo.

56. I have used the past tense in translating Apollo's reference to Athena's vote here, since a reference to an actual vote that Apollo has seen would mean that *ôrthôsen* is not a what philologists call a 'gnomic aorist;' that is, a category of a past tense verb that denotes a general maxim, not an actual situation. The almost universal tendency of scholars of this play not to imagine it performed has led to the assump-tion that Apollo does not refer to votes he has seen cast.

57. Sommerstein, *Aeschylus: Eumenides*, 223. Seaford ('Historiciz-ing Tragic Ambivalence, 210-1) rejects the arguments of Gagarin and Sommerstein that Athena's vote is clearly included in the 'equal num-ber', yet Seaford himself relies on a claim that 'these points have no weight, once it is realized that the audience is already familiar with the mechanism of 'the vote of Athena, instituted in the very first homicide trial, to resolve the problems of a tied vote'. However, the evidence for the 'vote of Athena' is itself relatively late, and thus not completely reliable, and a closer look at Seaford's footnote on this sentence (n. 23) yields this concession: 'This familiarity cannot be proved, but it is very likely.'

The concept of the 'casting' vote is central to the argument of Hester, 'Casting Vote', against Gagarin, 'Vote', especially 122-4. In addition to these intelligent, yet opposing, analyses, I would recom-mend Winnington-Ingram, *Studies*, especially 125 n. 110 (the revised version of 'Clytemnestra and the Vote of Athena'), who, 'after much hesitation', decides that Athena does not vote with the jury.

58. Sommerstein, *Aeschylus: Eumenides,* 234.

59. On hero cult see Burkert, *Greek Religion*, 203-8.

60. Hester, 'Casting Vote', 270.

61. Taplin (*Stagecraft*, 403-7) examines the basic problem of Apollo's exit thoroughly. Sommerstein (*Aeschylus: Eumenides,* 234) also notices that the entire content of Orestes' speech, which neglects Apollo, suggests a departure by Apollo before it begins. Scott ('Lines', 265) suggests Apollo remains, silent, until the end, but this seems the least preferable option, given the rancour his presence would cause the Furies.

62. Most, 'Apollo's' Last Words',13-15.

63. See Sommerstein's comments on these lines.

64. Bacon, 'Furies', 48 and 52.

65. On the song and its relationship to speech in this scene see Scott, *Musical Design*, 129-33.

66. Taplin, *Stagecraft*, 407-8 and Sommerstein, *Aeschylus: Eumenides,* 239-40.

67. Seaford ('Historicizing Tragic Ambivalence', 210) is quite abrupt and ungrounded in his assertion that 'the wrath of the Furies when it comes is not directed against Athena'. But the Furies verbally attack Athena in their first lines and threaten Athens physically because they know they cannot harm the goddess.

68. Griffith, 'Brilliant Dynasts', 101 n. 126: 'This rare expression is usually glossed over as just one more of the many words for "trampling" that run throughout the trilogy ... but it may derive extra force from the aristocratic associations of horse-riding, as of an infantry unit being "overrun" by cavalry ... or a crowd of pedestrians in the street being "trampled" under the hooves of upper-class riders.'

69. Hammond, 'More on Conditions', 30.

70. Compare Zeus' promise of new honours to Demeter in the *Hymn to Demeter* 441-4, to Athena's to the Furies in *Eumenides* at 807, 853-7.

71. On persuasion/*peithô* in the *Oresteia*, see Goldhill, *Language*, 44; McClure, *Spoken Like a Woman*, 70-111; and Buxton, *Persuasion*, 105-14.

72. In my article, 'Marriage', I made much of the elision of Athena from the Cassandra story; that elision would now seem to be part of this process of reserving Athena for her saving role in the *Eumenides*, outside the sordid world of the *Agamemnon*.

73. Gagarin (*Aeschylean Drama*, 115 and 210 n. 12) cites the connection between *Agamemnon* 1 and *Eumenides* 83.

74. Scott, *Musical Design*, 130-3. Scott also observes (152) that dactyls were the metre Calchas used in *Agamemnon* for his prophecy of virgin sacrifice. On the lecythion metre also see Chiasson, 'Lecythia', especially 16-21.

75. See Sommerstein, *Aeschylus: Eumenides,* 281 and Brown, 'Eumenides'.

76. Here Meineck's translation, again based on the experience of the *Oresteia* in the theatre, gets it right: 'Rejoice!'

77. On the composition of the participants in the final procession, see Sommerstein, *Aeschylus: Eumenides*, 275-8, who takes Athena's references to people and things far more literally than Taplin, *Stage-craft*, 411-15, who sometimes is so determined to do away with the idea of Aeschylean spectacle that he winds up overlooking its reality. Wiles, *Tragedy*, suggests that Taplin was overly influenced by the minimalist theatrical ethos of the 1960s.

78. See Haldane 'Musical Themes', on the *ololugê* cry in the *Oresteia.*

79. Sommerstein, *Aeschylus: Eumenides*, 285; McClure, *Spoken Like a Woman*, 110-11.

5. Justice, Law, and Athenian Politics in *Eumenides*

1. Ostracism was a tool for preserving democratic stability by allowing the Assembly to vote to exile temporarily an advocate for a contested policy, usually an aristocrat, who was thought to have become too powerful. The sources for the ostracism of Cimon include Thucydides 1.102.4 and Plutarch, *Cimon* 16-17. See the brief discussions in Ostwald, *Popular Sovereignty*, 17-18 and 179-80.

2. Macleod, 'Politics'.

3. An excellent introduction to and thorough overview of equality, freedom and law in Athens is Ostwald, *Popular Sovereignty.*

4. For a full discussion of the ambiguities of *dikê* in the *Oresteia*, see Goldhill, *Reading Greek Tragedy*, 33-56.

5. Podlecki, *Aeschylus: Eumenides*, 43.

6. Goldhill, *Reading Greek Tragedy*, 30.

7. Goldhill, for example (*Reading Greek Tragedy*, 56), stresses the irresolution of meaning at the end of *Eumenides*: 'The problem of *dikê* in this trilogy and its critical readings is not solved but endlessly repeated'. This stance is sharply criticized by Seaford, 'Historicizing Tragic Ambivalence'. In response, see Goldhill, 'Civic Ideology'.

8. For a succinct summary of the Athenian legal system, with references to primary sources, see Sommerstein, *Aeschylus: Eumenides*, 15-17. On Athenian law and murder in general, see Gagarin, *Early* and MacDowell, *Law.*

9. On Ephialtes' reforms and democracy see Aristotle, *The Athenian Constitution* 25-6; Jones, 'Role of Ephialtes'; Wallace, *Areopagos Council*; and Ostwald, *Popular Sovereignty*, 70-3 and 175-6.

10. On Pericles and Aeschylus, see Rosenbloom, *Aeschylus: Persians*, 16-17.

11. For detailed discussion of Ephialtes reforms and Oresteia, see Bowie, 'Religion'; Dover, 'Political Aspect'; Dodds, 'Morals'; Goldhill, 'Civic Ideology'; Jones, 'Role of Ephialtes', 69-74; Macleod, 'Politics'; Podlecki, *Political Background*, 80-100; Schaps, 'Aeschylus' Politics'. Bowie usefully summarizes the widely divergent interpretations of Aeschylean politics.

12. Cole (*'Oresteia'*) argues that Aeschylus in the *Oresteia* is favourable towards Cimon. But Cimon, it should be noted, is often more linked to the young Sophocles. Rhodes (*Commentary*, 312) sees an Aeschylus nervous about the reforms and concerned that the democrats might really get out of hand soon. For a broader conception of the persistence of oligarchic ideas in the *Oresteia*, see Griffith, 'Brilliant Dynasts'.

13. Schaps thus agrees with Sommerstein, *Aeschylus: Eumenides*, 218.

14. Bacon, 'Furies', 48 and 52.

15. The original, and still classic, treatment of the exodus and the Panathenaia is Headlam, 'The Last Scene'.

16. There is some dispute over who sings the final stanza. See Sommerstein (*Aeschylus: Eumenides*, 282-3) on lines 1023-47.

6. The Reception of *Eumenides*: Ancient Tragedy, Gender, and the Modern World

1. Zeitlin, 'Redeeming Matricide', provides a stimulating overview of the relationship of Euripidean drama to the *Oresteia*. On *Orestes* in particular, see Zeitlin, 'Closet'. On *Hecuba* and the *Oresteia*, see Thalmann, 'Euripides'.

2. On *Oedipus at Colonus* and the *Oresteia* see Winnington-Ingram, 'Religious Function'; Segal, *Tragedy*, 362-408; Brown, 'Eumenides', 276-81; and Lardinois, 'Greek Myths'.

3. Segal, *Tragedy*, 405.

4. For details on the Roman sources, see Podlecki, *Aeschylus: Eumenides*, 21-5.

5. On Aeschylus and the Germans see Ewans, *Wagner*, and Silk and Stern, *Nietzsche*. Goldhill (*Aeschylus* 88-90) has an excellent concise summary of the *Oresteia*'s reception in modern intellectual history.

6. Lattimore, *Aeschylus*, 30 and Thomson, *Aeschylus*. On the myth of the myth of matriarchy in the *Oresteia*, see Zeitlin's classic essay 'Dynamics', especially 89-98. See also Goldhill, *Reading Greek Tragedy*, 51-6.

7. Millet, *Sexual*, 114-15.

8. Goldhill, *Reading Greek Tragedy*, 54.

9. Winnington-Ingram, *Studies*, 101-31. More recently see Zeitlin, *Dynamics*; Foley, *Female*; and McClure, *Spoken*, 70-112. Goldhill (*Oresteia*, 33-41) provides an excellent brief introduction to the study of gender in the *Oresteia*.

10. Goldhill, *Oresteia*, 38.

11. Zeitlin, 'Dynamics', 87.

12. Zeitlin, 'Dynamics', 114.

13. Zeitlin, 'Dynamics', 113.

14. Goldhill, *Oresteia*, 40.

15. Winnington-Ingram, 'Clytemnestra and the Vote of Athena', 101-31 in *Studies*. See also Goldhill, *Oresteia*, 40 and *Reading Greek Tragedy*, 31.

16. McClure, *Spoken Like a Woman*, 106.

17. McClure, *Spoken Like a Woman*, 111.

18. For details on the ancient sources and the credibility of the argument, see Podlecki, *Aeschylus: Eumenides*, 178, and Sommerstein, *Aeschylus: Eumenides* 206-7. Winnington-Ingram, *Studies* 122-4, remains compelling reading on this subject, as does Zeitlin, 'Dynamics', 107-11.

19. Bacon, 'Furies', 52.

20. Bacon, 'Furies', 56.

21. A substantial paper comparing Xenakis and Aeschylus, by Evaggelia Vagopoulou of the Music Department, University of Bristol, is available online:
http://cicm.mshparisnord.org/ColloqueXenakis/papers/Vaggopoulou.pdf

22. Bourguereau's painting is on the cover of this book. Sargent's can be seen on the cover of Lloyd, *Oxford Readings*.

23. Eliot, *Poetry*, 30.

24. On the modern history of performance of Aeschylus, see Hall and Macintosh, *Greek Tragedy*, and Macintosh et al., *Agamemnon*.

25. This production was not a complete *Oresteia*, as some have written, but only its last play. It was reviewed in *The Musical Times*, vol. 27, no. 515 (1 January 1886), 23-4; this review is available at http://www.jstor.org. The text and musical score of the Cambridge *Eumenides* is now available through Google Books
http://books.google.com/books?id=89jYPQAACAAJ&dq=eumenides&source=gbs_book_other_versions_r&cad=5

Guide to Further Reading

Translations

Eumenides is always bundled with translations of the entire *Oresteia*. The modern reader has an embarrassment of riches in English editions. I shall here offer brief comments on a number of the translations listed in the bibliography below. Collard's edition is a prose translation, very reliable and with excellent notes. Ewans' version is based on his work in staging and contains an extensive 'theatrical commentary'. Fagles has many admirers, but I feel it has not aged well and contains at times too much Fagles. Tony Harrison's translation was written for the landmark production in masks at the National Theatre, London, in 1981; a video is available through Films for the Humanities. It condenses some aspects of the poetry and action and is particularly characterized by its restless rhythms, brilliant new metaphors, and often brutal alliterations. Ted Hughes' *Oresteia* is noteworthy for its fine versification. Lattimore's classic Chicago translation is now over a half-century old and lacks much in the way of help to the reader. Lloyd-Jones' edition is remarkably readable and includes a commentary by a truly great Hellenist. Meineck's accurate and lively translation keeps its lines corresponding to the Greek and is based on his own theatre work; Foley's introduction is concise and informative. More recently Shapiro and Burian combine the skills of a fine poet and outstanding scholar. Slavitt's edition is freer than most and lacks the support materials needed by most modern readers. Most recently, Sommerstein's splendid new Loeb edition offers an accurate and readable translation, an authoritative new Greek text, and copious notes. Of these translations of the *Oresteia*, I believe that the editions of Meineck and Shapiro/Burian have the most to offer, with Collard fine for those who do not mind prose translations.

Greek myth and religion

The standard starting place for the study of Greek religion is Burkert's *Greek Religion*. To learn more about bloodguilt and religious pollution, see Parker's *Miasma*. Dodds' older *The Greeks and the Irrational*

139

remains a valuable study of Greek religious psychology. Johnston's fascinating book, *Restless Dead: Encounters Between the Living and Dead in Ancient Greece*, deals extensively with matters such as hero cult, and its last chapter focuses on the Furies. For the myths on which Aeschylus drew, see Gantz, *Early Greek Myth: A Guide to Literary and Artistic Sources*. For the relationship between myth and ritual in Greek literature, I find valuable and continually illuminating the essays in Gould's *Myth, Ritual, Memory, and Exchange* and Vernant and Vidal-Naquet's *Myth and Tragedy in Ancient Greece*. The latter had an enormous influence on the work on Greek tragedy of Zeitlin, Goldhill and Foley which I discuss below.

Works on the Greek theatre and tragedy

Csapo/Slater's *The Context of Ancient Drama* is an invaluable tool for learning about the Greek theatre and festivals. Pickard-Cambridge, *The Dramatic Festivals of Athens*, is the standard scholarly account, but most students and teachers will find Csapo/Slater easier to use. In recent decades some of the most exciting work on Greek tragedy has involved its festival context and relation to the polis of Athens. On these topics (and others), see Easterling (ed.), *The Cambridge Companion to Greek Tragedy*, and Winkler and Zeitlin (eds), *Nothing to Do With Dionysos? Athenian Drama in its Social Context*. An excellent guide to all aspects of Greek tragedy is Gregory (ed.), *A Companion to Greek Tragedy*. Goldhill's *Reading Greek Tragedy* presents a provocative overview, influenced by literary theory, of most of the greatest Greek tragedies.

The reader is well served now with respect to many different aspects of Greek tragedy. There has also been much important and fascinating work in recent decades on the performance of Greek tragedy in Athens. This movement began in earnest with Taplin's *The Stagecraft of Aeschylus* and *Greek Tragedy in Action*. The former is intended at a highly specialized audience, but the latter is an excellent starting point, as is Wiles' *Greek Theatre Performance*, Ley's *A Short Introduction to the Ancient Greek Theatre* and Rehm's *Greek Tragic Theatre*. Also important are the more advanced recent works: Wiles' *Tragedy in Athens* and Ley's *The Theatricality of Greek Tragedy*. Central to the study of Greek tragedy recently has also been feminist interpretation; see Foley's *Female Acts*, Zeitlin's *Playing the Other* and McClure's *Spoken Like a Woman*.

Aeschylus

Herington, *Aeschylus*, is a brief overview that has aged very well since its publication. Other vintage overviews that still offer much include Winnington-Ingram, *Studies in Aeschylus*, and Gagarin, *Aeschylean*

Drama. Lebeck, *The Oresteia: A Study in Language and Structure*, is a nuanced account of the trilogy's language and imagery. Many will find useful Conacher's *Aeschylus' Oresteia: A Literary Commentary*. Those interested in matters such as the Ephialtic reforms should start with Podlecki's *The Political Background of Aeschylean Tragedy*. The recent *Oxford Readings in Classical Studies: Aeschylus*, edited by Lloyd, contains a number of very important articles on Aeschylus and the *Oresteia*. As noted above, Taplin's *The Stagecraft of Aeschylus* is fundamental, but mainly for readers who already have a thorough grounding in Greek tragedy and Aeschylus. Goldhill has written two books on the *Oresteia. Language, Sexuality, Narrative: The Oresteia* is a revision of his dissertation, and highly influenced by Deconstruction. Like Taplin's book, this one is for experienced readers only. However, his briefer book, *The Oresteia*, is incisive, insightful and readable by almost anyone who wants to learn more about the trilogy. Rosenmeyer's *The Art of Aeschylus* will also reward primarily the more experienced student of Aeschylus. Anyone interested in the Aeschylean chorus should consult Scott's *Musical Design in Aeschylean Theater*, which makes the music of Greek tragedy surprisingly accessible to non-specialists. At the time of the writing, Peter Burian of Duke University had begun to assemble a volume in Blackwell's Companion series that will feature essays by many of the world's leading scholars on Aeschylus.

Bibliography

Abbreviations

AJP = *American Journal of Philology*
CJ = *Classical Journal*
ClAnt = *Classical Antiquity*
CP = *Classical Philology*
CQ = *Classical Quarterly*
G&R = *Greek and Rome*
GRBS = *Greek, Roman and Byzantine Studies*
HSCP = *Harvard Studies in Classical Philology*
JHS = *Journal of Hellenic Studies*
PCPS = *Proceedings of the Cambridge Philological Association*
TAPA = *Transactions of the American Philological Association*

Greek texts with English commentaries

Podlecki, A.J. (ed. and tr.) *Aeschylus: Eumenides* (Warminster: Aris and Phillips, 1989).

Sommerstein, A.H. (ed.) *Aeschylus: Eumenides* (Cambridge: Cambridge University Press, 1989).

Translations

Collard, C. *Aeschylus, Oresteia* (Oxford: Oxford University Press, 2002).

Ewans, M. *Aischylos, The Oresteia* (London: Everyman, 1995).

Fagles, R. *Aeschylus, The Oresteia* (New York: Penguin, 1966), with introduction and commentary by W.B. Stanford.

Harrison, T. *The Oresteia* (London: Collings, 1982).

Hughes, T. *The Oresteia* (New York: Farrar, Straus, Giroux, 1999).

Lattimore, R. *Aeschylus I: Oresteia* (Chicago: University of Chicago Press, 1953).

Lloyd-Jones, H. *Aeschylus: The Oresteia* (London: Duckworth, 1979), includes commentary.

Bibliography

Meineck, P. *Aeschylus, Oresteia* (Indianapolis: Hackett, 1998), with introduction by Helene Foley.

Shapiro, A., and P. Burian. *Aeschylus, The Oresteia* (Oxford: Oxford University Press, 2003), with introduction and commentary by Burian.

Slavitt, D. *Aeschylus, 1: The Oresteia* (Philadelphia: University of Pennsylvania Press, 1998), with introduction by Palmer Bovie.

Sommerstein, Alan H. *Aeschylus II: Agamemnon, Libation-Bearers, Eumenides* (Cambridge, Mass.: Harvard University Press, 2008).

Articles and books

I have listed here only works written in English that are readily available and, for the most part, intelligible without a knowledge of Greek.

Bachofen, J.J. *Myth, Religion and Mother-Right: Selected Writings*, tr. R. Manheim, Bollingen series 84 (Princeton: Princeton University Press, 1967).

Bacon, H. 'The Furies' Homecoming', *CP* 96 (2001) 48-59.

Belfiore, E. *Tragic Pleasures: Aristotle on Plot and Emotion* (Princeton: Princeton University Press, 1992).

———. *Murder among Friends: Violations of* Philia *in Greek Tragedy* (Oxford: Oxford University Press, 2000).

Boegehold, A.L. 'A Signifying Gesture: Euripides, *Iphigenia Taurica*, 955-66', *JHS* 93 (1989) 81-3.

Bowie, A.M. 'Religion and Politics in Aeschylus' *Oresteia*', *CQ* 43 (1993) 10-13, repr. in Lloyd, *Oxford Readings*, 323-58.

Brown, A.L. 'Some Problems in the *Eumenides* of Aeschylus', *JHS* 102 (1982) 26-32.

———. 'The Erinyes in the *Oresteia*: Real Life, the Supernatural, and the Stage', *JHS* 103 (1983) 13-34.

———. 'Eumenides in Greek Tragedy', *CQ* 34 (1984) 260-81.

Burkert, W. *Greek Religion* (Cambridge, Mass.: Harvard University Press, 1985).

Buxton, R.G.A. *Persuasion in Greek Tragedy: A Study of Peitho* (Cambridge: Cambridge University Press, 1982).

Chiasson, C. 'Lecythia and the Justice of Zeus in Aeschylus' *Oresteia*', *Phoenix* 42 (1988) 1-21.

Cole, J.R. 'The *Oresteia* and Cimon', *HSCP* 81 (1977) 99-111.

Conacher, D.J. *Aeschylus' Oresteia: A Literary Commentary* (Toronto: University of Toronto Press, 1987).

Csapo, E. 'The Men Who Built the Theatres: *Theatropolai, Theatronai*, and the *Architektones*', in P. Wilson (ed.), *The Greek Theatre and Festivals* (Oxford: Oxford University Press, 2007), 87-149.

Bibliography

Csapo, E. and Slater, W. *The Context of Ancient Drama* (Ann Arbor: University of Michigan Press, 1995).

Dodds, E.R. *The Greeks and the Irrational* (Berkeley: University of California Press, 1951).

————. 'Morals and Politics in the *Oresteia*', *Proceedings of the Cambridge Philological Society* 6 (1960), 19-31, repr. in *The Ancient Concept of Progress* (Oxford. Oxford University Press, 1073) ch. 4, and again in Lloyd, *Oxford Readings*, 245-64.

Dover, K.J. 'The Political Aspect of Aeschylus' *Eumenides*', *JHS* 77 (1957) 230-7.

duBois, P. *Centaurs and Amazons: Women and the Pre-History of the Great Chain of Being* (Ann Arbor: University of Michigan Press, 1991).

Easterling, P.E. 'The Presentation of Character in Aeschylus', *G&R* 20 (1973) 3-19, repr. in I. McAuslan and P. Walcot (eds) *Greek Tragedy* (Oxford: Oxford University Press, 1993), 12-28.

Easterling, P.E., 'A Show for Dionysus', in Easterling, *Cambridge Companion*, 36-53.

————. (ed.) *The Cambridge Companion to Greek Tragedy* (Cambridge: Cambridge University Press, 1997).

Easterling, P.E. and B. Knox (eds). *The Cambridge History of Classical Literature,* vol. I: *Greek Literature* (Cambridge: Cambridge University Press, 1985).

Eliot, T.S. *Poetry and Drama* (London: Faber and Faber, 1952).

Ewans, M. 'Agamemnon at Aulis: A Study in the *Oresteia*', *Ramus* 4 (1975) 1-15.

————. *Wagner and Aeschylus: The Ring and the Oresteia* (London: Faber and Faber, 1982).

Faraone, C.A. 'Aeschylus' ὕμνος δέσμιος (*Eum.* 306) and Attic Judicial Curse Tablets', *JHS* 105 (1985) 150-4.

Foley, H.P. *Female Acts in Greek Tragedy* (Princeton: Princeton University Press, 2001).

Fontenrose, J. 'Gods and Men in the *Oresteia*', *TAPA* 102 (1971) 71-109.

Fraenkel, E. *Aeschylus: Agamemnon*, 3 vols (Oxford: Clarendon Press, 1950).

Gagarin, M. 'The Vote of Athena', *AJP* 96 (1975) 121-7.

————. *Aeschylean Drama* (Berkeley: University of California Press, 1976).

————. *Early Greek Law* (Berkeley: University of California Press, 1986).

Gantz, T.N. 'The Aischylean Tetralogy: Attested and Conjectured Groups', *AJP* 101 (1980) 133-64, repr. with revisions in Lloyd, *Readings*, 40-70.

————. 'The Fires of the Oresteia', *JHS* 97 (1977) 28-38.

Bibliography

————. *Early Greek Myth: A Guide to Literary and Artistic Sources* (Baltimore: Johns Hopkins University Press, 1993).

Goldhill, S. *Language, Sexuality, Narrative: The Oresteia* (Cambridge: Cambridge University Press, 1984).

————. *Reading Greek Tragedy* (Cambridge: Cambridge University Press, 1986).

————. 'The Great Dionysia and Civic Ideology', in Winkler and Zeitlin, *Nothing*, 97-129.

————. *The Oresteia* (Cambridge: Cambridge University Press, 1992; 2nd edn 2004).

————. 'The Audience of Greek Tragedy', in Easterling, *Cambridge Companion*, 54-68.

————. 'The Language of Tragedy: Rhetoric and Communication', in Easterling, *Cambridge Companion*, 127-50.

————. 'Civic Ideology and the Problem of Difference: The Politics of Aeschylean Tragedy, Once Again', *JHS* 120 (2000) 34-56.

Gould, J. 'Tragedy in Performance', in Easterling and B.M.W. Knox (eds), *Cambridge History*, 6-29, reprinted in Gould, *Myth*, 174-202.

————. *Myth, Ritual, Memory, and Exchange: Essays in Greek Literature and Culture* (Oxford: Oxford University Press, 2001).

Goward, B. *Aeschylus: Agamemnon* (London: Duckworth, 2005).

Gregory, J. (ed.) *A Companion to Greek Tragedy* (Oxford: Blackwell, 2005).

Griffith, M. 'Brilliant Dynasts: Power and Politics in the *Oresteia*', *ClAnt* 14 (1995) 62-129.

————. 'Slaves of Dionysos: Satyrs, Audience, and the Ends of the *Oresteia*', *ClAnt* 21 (2002) 195-258.

Haldane, J.A. 'Musical Themes and Imagery in Aeschylus', *JHS* 85 (1965) 33-41.

Hall, E. *Inventing the Barbarian* (Oxford: Oxford University Press, 1989).

Hall, E. and F. Macintosh. *Greek Tragedy and the British Theatre, 1660-1914* (Oxford: Oxford University Press, 2005).

Hammond, N.G.L. 'The Conditions of Dramatic Production to the Death of Aeschylus', *GRBS* 13 (1972) 387-450.

————. 'More on the Conditions of Dramatic Production to the Death of Aeschylus', *GRBS* 29 (1988) 5-33.

Headlam, W. 'The Last Scene of the *Eumenides*', *JHS* 26 (1906) 268-77.

Henderson, J. 'Women and the Athenian Dramatic Festivals', *TAPA* 121 (1991) 133-47.

Herington, C.J. *Poetry into Drama: Early Tragedy and the Greek Poetic Tradition* (Berkeley: University of California Press, 1985).

————. *Aeschylus* (New Haven: Yale University Press, 1986).

Hester, D.A. 'The Casting Vote', *AJP* 102 (1981) 265-74.

Bibliography

Himmelhoch, L. 'Athena's Entrance at *Eumenides* 405 and Hippotrophic Imagery in the *Oresteia*', *Arethusa* 38 (2005) 263-302.

Ireland, S. *Aeschylus* (Oxford: Oxford University Press, 1986).

Johnston, S.I. *Restless Dead: Encounters Between the Living and the Dead in Ancient Greece* (Berkeley: University of California Press, 1999).

Jones, J. *On Aristotle and Greek Tragedy* (New York: Oxford University Press, 1962).

Jones, L.A. 'The Role of Ephialtes in the Rise of Athenian Democracy', *ClAnt* 6 (1987) 53-76.

Knox, B.M.W. 'Aeschylus and the Third Actor', *AJP* 93 (1972) 104-24, repr. in *Word and Action: Essays on the Ancient Theater* (Baltimore: Johns Hopkins University Press, 1979), 39-55.

Lardinois, A. 'Greek Myths for Athenian Rituals: Religion and Politics in Aeschylus' *Eumenides* and Sophocles' *Oedipus Coloneus*', *GRBS* 33 (1992) 313-37.

Lebeck, A. *The Oresteia: A Study in Language and Structure* (Cambridge, Mass.: Harvard University Press, 1971).

Lefkowitz, M.R. *The Lives of the Greek Poets* (London: Duckworth, 1981).

Ley, G. *A Short Introduction to the Ancient Greek Theatre* (Chicago: University of Chicago Press, 2006).

———. *The Theatricality of Greek Tragedy: Playing Space and Chorus* (Chicago: University of Chicago Press, 2007).

Lloyd, M. (ed.) *Oxford Readings in Aeschylus* (Oxford: Oxford University Press, 2007).

Lloyd-Jones, H. *The Justice of Zeus* (Berkeley: University of California Press, 1971).

MacDowell, D.M. *The Law in Classical Athens* (Ithaca: Cornell University Press, 1978).

Macintosh, F., Michelakis, P., Hall, E. and Taplin, O. (eds) *Agamemnon in Performance 458 BC to AD 2004* (Oxford: Oxford University Press, 2005).

Macleod, C. 'Politics and the *Oresteia*', *JHS* 102 (1982) 124-44, repr. in his *Collected Papers* (Oxford 1983) ch. 3, and again in Lloyd, *Oxford Readings*, 265-301.

McClure, L. *Spoken Like a Woman: Speech and Gender in Athenian Drama* (Princeton: Princeton University Press, 1999).

Marshall, C.W. 'Casting the *Oresteia*', *CJ* 98 (2003) 257-74.

Millett, K. *Sexual Politics* (New York: Ballantine, 1978).

Mitchell-Boyask, R.N. 'The Marriage of Cassandra and the *Oresteia*: Text, Image, Performance', *TAPA* 136 (2006) 269-97.

———. *Plague and the Athena Imagination: Drama, History, and the Cult of Asclepius* (Cambridge: Cambridge University Press, 2008).

Bibliography

Most, G. 'Apollo's Last Words in Aeschylus' *Eumenides*', *CQ* 56 (2006) 12-18.

Nussbaum, M.C. *The Fragility of Goodness: Luck and Ethics in Greek Tragedy and Philosophy* (Cambridge: Cambridge University Press, 1986).

Ostwald, M. *From Popular Sovereignty to the Sovereignty of Law: Law, Society and Politics in Fifth-Century Athens* (Berkeley: University of California Press, 1986).

Pickard-Cambridge, A.W. *The Dramatic Festivals of Athens*; 2nd edn, revised by J. Gould and D.M. Lewis, reissued with supplement and corrections (Oxford: Clarendon Press, 1968).

Parker, R. *Miasma: Pollution and Purification in Early Greek Religion* (New York: Oxford University Press, 1990).

Peradotto, J. 'Some Patterns of Nature Imagery in the *Oresteia*', *AJP* 85 (1964) 378-93.

———. 'Cledonomancy in the *Oresteia*', *AJP* 90 (1969) 1-21.

Podlecki, A.J. *The Political Background of Aeschylean Tragedy* (Ann Arbor: University of Michigan Press: 1967).

Quincey, J.H. 'Orestes and the Argive Alliance', *CQ* 14 (1964) 190-206.

Rabinowitz, N.S. 'From Force to Persuasion: Aeschylus' *Oresteia* as Cosmogonic Myth', *Ramus* 10 (1981), 159-91.

Rehm, R. *Greek Tragic Theatre* (New York: Routledge, 1992).

———. 'The Staging of Suppliant Plays', *GRBS* 29 (1988) 263-307.

Rhodes, P.J. *A Commentary on the Aristotelian Athenaion Politeia* (Oxford: Oxford University Press, 1981).

———. (ed.) *Athenian Democracy* (Oxford: Oxford University Press, 2004).

Roberts, D. *Apollo and His Oracle in the Oresteia* (Göttingen: Vandenhoeck and Rupprecht, 1984).

Rosenbloom, D. *Aeschylus: Persians* (London: Duckworth, 2006).

Rosenmeyer, T.G. *The Art of Aeschylus* (Berkeley: University of California Press, 1982).

Saïd, S. 'Aeschylean Tragedy', in Gregory, *Companion*, 215-32.

Schaps, D.M. 'Aeschylus' Politics and the Theme of the *Oresteia*', in *Nomodeiktes: Greek Studies in Honor of Martin Ostwald* (Ann Arbor: University of Michigan Press, 1993), 505-15.

Scott, W. C. 'Lines for Clytemnestra (*Agamemnon* 489-502)', *TAPA* 108 (1982) 259-69.

Scott, W.C. *Musical Design in Aeschylean Theater* (Hanover: University Press of New England, 1984).

Scullion, S. *Three Studies in Athenian Dramaturgy* (Stuttgart and Leipzig: G.B. Teubner, 1994).

Seaford, R. *Reciprocity and Ritual: Homer and Tragedy in the Developing City-state* (Oxford: Oxford University Press, 1994).

———. 'Historicizing Tragic Ambivalence: The Vote of Athena', in B.

147

Bibliography

Goff (ed.) *History, Tragedy, Theory: Dialogues on Athenian Drama* (Austin: University of Texas Press, 1995), 202-21.

Segal, C. P. *Tragedy and Civilization: An Interpretation of Sophocles* (Cambridge, Mass.: Harvard University Press, 1981).

Sider, D. 'Stagecraft in the *Oresteia*', *AJP* 99 (1978) 12-27.

Silk, M.S. (ed.) *Tragedy and the Tragic: Greek Theatre and Beyond* (Oxford. Oxford University Press, 1996).

Silk, M.S. and J.P. Stern. *Nietzsche on Tragedy* (Cambridge: Cambridge University Press, 1981).

Solmsen, F. *Hesiod and Aeschylus* (Ithaca: Cornell University Press, 1949).

Sommerstein, A.H. *Aeschylean Tragedy* (Bari: Levante, 1996).

Taplin, O. *The Stagecraft of Aeschylus* (Oxford: Clarendon Press, 1977).

———. *Greek Tragedy in Action* (Berkeley: University of California Press, 1978).

Thalmann, W.G. 'Euripides and Aeschylus: The Case of the *Hekabe*', *ClAnt* 12 (1993) 126-59.

Thomson, G. *Aeschylus and Athens* (London: Lawrence & Wishart, 1946).

Tyrrell, W.B. *Amazons: A Study in Athenian Mythmaking* (Baltimore: Johns Hopkins University Press, 1984).

Tyrrell, W.B. and F.S. Brown. *Athenian Myths and Institutions: Words in Action* (Oxford: Oxford University Press, 1991).

Vellacott, P. 'Has Good Prevailed? A Further Study of the *Oresteia*', *HSCP* 81 (1977) 113-22.

Vidal-Naquet, P. 'Hunting and Sacrifice in Aeschylus' *Oresteia*', in J.-P. Vernant and P. Vidal-Naquet, *Myth and Tragedy in Ancient Greece*, tr. J. Lloyd (New York: Zone Books, 1988), 141-60.

Wallace, R.W. *The Areopagos Council, to 307 B.C.* (Baltimore: Johns Hopkins University Press, 1989).

West, M.L. 'The Prometheus Trilogy', *JHS* 99 (1979) 130-48, repr. in Lloyd, *Oxford Readings*, 359-96.

Wiles, D. *Tragedy in Athens: Performance Space and Theatrical Meaning* (Cambridge: Cambridge University Press, 1997).

———. *Greek Theatre Performance: An Introduction* (Cambridge: Cambridge University Press, 2000).

Winkler, J. and Zeitlin, F. (eds) *Nothing to Do With Dionysos? Athenian Drama in its Social Context* (Princeton: Princeton University Press, 1990).

Winnington-Ingram, R.P. 'A Religious Function of Greek Tragedy: A Study in the *Oedipus at Colonus* and the *Oresteia*', *JHS* 74 (1954) 16-24.

———. *Studies in Aeschylus* (Cambridge: Cambridge University Press, 1983).

Bibliography

————. 'Aeschylus', in Easterling and Knox (eds) *Cambridge History*, 281-95.

————. 'The Origins of Tragedy', in Easterling and Knox (eds) *Cambridge History*, 1-6.

Zeitlin, F.I. 'The Motif of the Corrupted Sacrifice in the *Oresteia*', *TAPA* 96 (1965) 463-508.

————. 'The Dynamics of Misogyny: Myth and Mythmaking in the *Oresteia*', in *Playing the Other: Gender And Society in Classical Greek Literature* (Chicago: University of Chicago Press, 1996), 87-119, repr. with revisions from *Arethusa* 11.1-2 (1978) 149-84.

————. 'The Closet of Masks: Role Playing and Mythmaking in the *Orestes* of Euripides', *Ramus* 9 (1980) 51-77.

————. 'Redeeming Matricide: Euripides Rereads the *Oresteia*' in V. Pedrick and S. Oberhelman (eds), *The Soul of Tragedy: Essays in Athenian Drama* (Chicago: University of Chicago Press, 2005), 199-226.

Glossary

Anapaest: a poetic metre (two short syllables followed by a long) associated with marching and thus often used for entrances and exits, especially by the *choros*.

Archon: a city official who was elected for a one-year term, nine each year, from a small group of wealthy and well-known families. Only one term was allowed to each archon, after which he could serve on the Areopagus. One archon was responsible for deciding which playwrights would be granted a chorus and thus be allowed to participate in the City Dionysia.

Chorêgos: the financing producer for each playwright, with the principal responsibility of funding the chorus.

Choros: a group of twelve men who sang and danced, wearing costume and masks, on a single day of performances of three tragedies and a satyr play.

Dactyl: a poetic metre that consisted of a long syllable followed by two short ones, most commonly used for heroic epic poetry.

Dithyramb: a choral poem sung in honour of Dionysus, sometimes believed to be one of the sources of tragic drama.

Dochmaic: a poetic metre, exclusively lyric, associated with excitement and intense joy or grief.

Ekkyklêma: the flat, wheeled cart that could be quickly rolled out from inside the *skênê* to show what has happened inside (such as corpses following a murder).

Iambic: a poetic metre, consisting of a short syllable followed by a long, used for normal speech by characters.

Lecythion: a stately poetic metre associated in the *Oresteia* with the justice of Zeus.

Mêchanê: a crane, stationed by the *skênê*, with an attached platform, which could be used to bring characters, almost invariably gods, swiftly into the acting area.

Metic: a foreigner given permission to reside in Athens.

Omphalos: literally, 'the navel', this term refers to the stone Rhea gave to Cronus to eat in place of Zeus, who was then hidden in Crete until Cronus disgorged Zeus' siblings. Zeus then placed the stone in Delphi, where it was regarded as the centre of the earth.

Orchêstra: the circular area in between the *skênê* and the audience where the *choros* sang and danced. Actors sometimes occupied this area as well.

Parodos: either one of the two side entrances (also known as *eisodoi*), or the first song of the *choros* as it entered the *orchêstra*.

Satyr play: the final of the four dramas each day during the City Dionysia, a humorous play with a *choros* dressed as satyrs (a mythical creature, half man and half goat).

Skênê: literally 'the tent', at the back of the acting area, a small structure invented just before the production of the *Oresteia* whose front consisted of panels painted to represent the drama's 'scene'.

Stasimon: a choral ode sang after the *parodos*, and in between episodes.

Stichomythia: exhanges between two characters consisting of single lines, used to represent rapid-fire debate.

Tragoidia: literally, 'the goat song', the origin of our word tragedy. The source of this word is thought to be a goat given to the prize-winning poet early in the history of the Athenian theatre.

Theatron: 'the seeing place', the bowl on the south slope of the Acropolis where the audience sat.

Chronology

534 BC	Contests in *tragoidia* instituted at the Athenian City Dionysia.
525/4	Birth of Aeschylus.
510	Expulsion of the Peisistratid tyrants from Athens.
508/7	Cleisthenes institutes democracy.
499/8	Aeschylus debuts as tragedian.
490	First Persian invasion; Athenians defeat Persians at Marathon; Aeschylus fights.
484	First victory of Aeschylus.
480-79	Second Persian invasion, led by King Xerxes. Battles of Thermopylae, Salamis and Plataea. Aeschylus present at Salamis.
478	Formation of the Delian League.
472	Aeschylus wins first prize with the tetralogy, *Phineus, Persians, Glaukus of Potniae*, and *Prometheus Pyrkaeus*.
472-69	Aeschylus visits Sicily at some point during these years and produces *Persians* and *The Women of Aetna*; this visit could have also occurred 476/5, but without the *Persians*.
468	Sophocles debuts and defeats Aeschylus.
467	Aeschylus wins first prize with the tetralogy, *Laius, Oedipus, Seven against Thebes*, and *Sphinx*.
463(?)	Aeschylus wins first prize with the tetralogy, *Suppliant Women, Aegyptians, Danaids, Amymone*.
462	Reform of the Areopagus Council by Ephialtes, Athenian alliance with Argos.
461	Assassination of Ephialtes.
458	Aeschylus wins first prize with the tetralogy, *Agamemnon, Libation Bearers, Eumenides*, and *Proteus* (together later known as *Oresteia*).

152

Chronology

456/5   Death of Aeschylus at Gela in Sicily.
455   Euripides debuts.
1518 AD   Publication of first printed edition of Aeschylus, the
              Aldine, in Venice.

Modern performance history

The list below contains only distinct performances of *Eumenides*
outside the entire *Oresteia*. It has been culled from the APGRD database (Archive of Performances of Greek and Roman Drama,
http://www.apgrd.ox.ac.uk/), compiled by Amanda Wrigley. The
APGRD database contains 208 separate entries for the entire *Oresteia*.

1885   *Eumenides* in ancient Greek, with music composed by
              Stanford, at the University of Cambridge.
1886   *Eumenides* in English at Beloit College, Wisconsin.
1898-99   *Eumenides* in English at Buffalo Opera House,
              Carnegie Lyceum in New York, and Point Loma,
              California.
1901   *Eumenides* in English at Point Loma, California;
              inauguration of new Greek theatre. Repeated in 1922,
              1925, 1927.
1907   New performance of the 1885 Cambridge production
              at the University of California, Berkeley.
1932   *Eumenides* in ancient Greek at Randolph-Macon
              Women's College, Lynchburg, Virginia.
1934   *Eumenides* in English at UCLA.
1953   *Eumenides* in ancient Greek at Randolph-Macon
              Women's College, Lynchburg, Virginia.
1960   *Libation Bearers* and *Eumenides* in modern Greek at
              the Piraeus Theatre, Athens.
1960   *Eumenides* in English in New York City by Living
              Theater Company.
1961   *Eumenides* in modern Greek in New York City.
1967   *Libation Bearers* and *Eumenides* in ancient Greek at
              Bradfield College, England.
1968   *Libation Bearers* and *Eumenides* as dance-dramas by
              Chorica Dance Company in New York City.
1973   *Eumenides* in ancient Greek at Wellesley College,
              Wellesley, Massachusetts.
1980   *Eumenides* in ancient Greek at Wellesley College,
              Wellesley, Massachusetts.

153

1986	Radio performance of *Eumenides* in Romania as part of a complete *Oresteia* series.
1986	*Eumenides* in modern Greek at Epidaurus, Greece.
1990	*Eumenides* in English at Tufts University, Medford, Massachusetts.
1993	*The Furies* in English at the University of California, Santa Cruz.
1994	Pasolini's adaptation of *Eumenides*, in Italian, as part of a complete *Oresteia,* over three months.
1995	*Eumenides* in English in New York City.
1996	*The Furies* in English at the Classics Greek Theatre of Oregon.
2001	*Eumenides* in English at the University of Dallas, Texas.
2001	*The Furies* in English by Ten Thousand Things in Santa Monica, California.
2004	*Eumenides* in English in New York City at the American Theater for Actors.
2005	*Eumenides* in Albanian in Athens, Greece.

The APGRD database also shows that Sartre's modern play based on *Eumenides, Les Mouches,* has been performed in 1941 (France), 1945 (Sweden), 1947 and 1951 (USA), and 1951 (England). Its English translation, *The Flies,* has been performed in England (1948, 1956), Japan (1961, 1974), USA (1965, 1997), South Africa (1972), and Canada (2003). Also according to the APGRD database Eliot's *The Family Reunion* has received performances only in Britain in 1939, 1954, 1956, 1961, 1979 and 1999.

Index

Index

Index